INTRODUCING
CHURCH GROWTH

INTRODUCING CHURCH GROWTH

A Textbook in Missions

by
Tetsunao Yamamori
and
E. LeRoy Lawson

A Division of Standard Publishing
Cincinnati, Ohio
40-002

Library of Congress Catalog Card Number: 74-24577

ISBN 0-87239-000-4

Foreword

Church growth, an idea whose time has come, is bursting across the American scene. Churches, denominations, and brotherhoods have suddenly become acutely conscious of their growth patterns. The cop-out, "We are not growing in numbers but we are in quality," sounds less convincing. Church growth seminars, workshops, books, and films are found everywhere. Conscience on communicating the gospel effectively has awakened. Colleges and seminaries are introducing courses on church growth.

Introducing Church Growth by Yamamori and Lawson applies growth thinking to American churches—large and small, urban and rural, downtown and suburban. This wide-ranging book should be owned by every church, read by every member of the board, and studied by youth and by women's organizations.

Church growth is everyone's business. The people of God are immersed in growing numbers of non-Christians right here in America, and ways—many ways—must be found in which the forty million or more who have never trusted Jesus, known abundant life, or been clothed in the righteousness of God, can become genuine parts of the Body. This book will come to Christians as does a breath of fresh air. Its competent discussion of the complex and exciting matter of growth will help many congregations break out of old, static patterns. Slow growth is a disease, fortunately curable. Studying this book is a first step in becoming a healthy growing, Spirit-filled church.

February 1, 1974

–*Donald McGavran*
School of Missions
Fuller Theological
Seminary
Pasadena, California

Preface

Within the past few years the explosion of church growth publications has been nothing short of phenomenal. At an increasing rate, in-depth case studies of churches, monographs and articles, theses and dissertations, theoretical studies and criticisms, and even journals are being published to insure church growth theory a rapidly expanding audience. These works have challenged mission thought as nothing else has since the famous Hocking-Kraemer debates of earlier decades.

Among these many publications one need has remained unfulfilled. Besides Donald A. McGavran's *Understanding Church Growth*, no introductory textbook for church growth studies has been written. The authors have prepared this volume to supply this need for a textbook for Bible college and seminary students, pastors, and mission leaders on the local and national levels.

Students should find in these pages a helpful introduction to the major thought and most important publications dealing with church growth today. Believing that the primary materials should speak for themselves whenever possible, the authors have selected generous excerpts from the wide variety of materials now available. The editorial comments, questions, and suggestions are to stimulate additional reading and research into the possibilities for the growth of the church in our times.

The authors also hope that American pastors will find the volume useful. Although by far the majority of church growth research has focused on the church in foreign lands, the authors are convinced that many situations and principles are analogous to the American church scene. They have, therefore, tried to select materials which suggest applications of church growth principles to local American congregations. Church growth in America can be fully understood only when viewed as a part of the total world church growth picture. We can be quite objective when analyzing a church's growth or stagnation in Korea, for example. It is not quite so easy to be objective about the growth or non-growth of "my home church." We too readily make excuses or defend bad judgment at home when our egos are involved. Perhaps it has been necessary, therefore, to develop tools and skills for church growth research by concentrating on studies of the church in traditional mission fields throughout the world. These research projects have yielded conclusions which apparently correspond to American church growth experience. Consequently, the alert minister, in reading case studies of church growth in Asia, Africa, and Latin America will find many circumstances paralleling his experience in America.

The authors have written with the dedicated layman in mind, also. The chairman or member of a local missions committee, struggling to make decisions on behalf of his congregation, needs guidance in weighing alternatives among the many requests for support he receives annually. The presupposition of this book is that all such requests need to be judged by church growth principles, with every congregation exercising wise stewardship over the limited resources available. To do "mission work" is not sufficient in these critical times. To make churches grow is the goal. Every mission dollar, therefore, must be prayerfully and intelligently dedicated to that end.

A word must be said about the format of this book. The authors have attempted to be suggestive, not exhaustive, in their treatment of the subject. Frequent references are made to other works for a fuller discussion of the materials introduced here. This book is designed to be a workbook, with the questions almost as important as the printed text. You are, therefore, invited to write in your book, to respond to the questions, to argue at will with the writers. The authors have stated a definite point of view, but there is room for disagreement. The Great Commission demands our most critical thinking. If the ideas presented in this book stimulate you to an independent but differing viewpoint, so much the better, as long as churches grow to the glory of Christ.

Introducing Church Growth serves both academic and non-academic audiences. On campus, it is a source book of primary materials, a workbook, a basis for discussion for several kinds of courses: Introduction to Christian Missions, Mission Theory and Practice, Research and Planning for Church Growth, Evangelism, Church Administration, Missionary Anthropology, Comparative Religions, and Introduction to Church Growth. In these courses, the textbook will lead the student "to do church growth" through suggested research projects.

Off campus, the book will assist missions committees and study groups, will guide the burdened pastor to new standards for determining the value of mission works, will aid church officers in financial and spiritual planning, and will serve as a basis for conferences and workshops and mission fairs. The individual Christian who desires to understand the modern missionary enterprises should find help on these pages. Further, he will be inspired as he learns what God has done through His church in many fields.

The reader will not have to study many of these pages before realizing the tremendous influence Dr. Donald McGavran has had upon church growth thinking generally and upon these authors specifically. In the popular mind, church growth thinking has been almost synonymous with McGavran thinking. Now that many able scholars are adding to church growth literature, this popular thinking is unfair to the magnitude of church growth influence in modern missions and to the excellent contributions of other church growth thinkers. But the popular mind is correct in attributing to Dr. McGavran great honor as the pioneer in the field. All of his students have been motivated by his insistence that the church must grow. The authors of this book share his conviction. We hope that *Introducing Church Growth* will contribute to the growth of your church.

Contents

PART I

WHAT IS CHURCH GROWTH?

Like all successful reform efforts, the church growth movement has its roots firmly planted in history. To the casual observer it may appear to be primarily a modern modification of traditional mission studies, adding its charts and graphs and case studies to missions libraries already filled with biographies and surveys and histories of missions. Some of its critics claim that its origin is found in the American preoccupation with progress and not in any profound understanding of New Testament teachings. But in spite of their adoption of modern scientific tools for measuring and encouraging growth, leaders in the movement insist that their inspiration is fundamentally Biblical. "Jesus founded no static organization," they emphasize. "He established a dynamic fellowship designed to draw every willing soul from every nation in the world into its circle. Jesus was not content with twelve disciples, or 120, or 3,000. He instructed His apostles, and through them, His church to go into all the nations, making disciples and baptizing and teaching in the name of the triune God. His earliest followers took His words seriously and His church grew amazingly. Such growth is possible today. The commission is the same, the need of men and women for the Savior is unchanged—yet the church is not enjoying the growth of the first century. Why?"

That *why* is what motivates the church growth movement and forces serious students of missions to restudy Biblical and historical accounts of those first centuries and every succeeding century. There have been periods of great growth and others of little or no growth. The question remains: in those stagnant centuries, what happened to the church? How did it lose its fire?

A few determined leaders in the sixteenth century asked that question. To find the answer they read their Bibles. That return to the church's origins ignited the great Protestant Reformation. A few equally determined missiologists, confident that the confusion of today's missionary enterprise can be overcome and a fantastic multiplying of Christian believers and congregations can happen in our time, have sparked a twentieth-century reformation of missions. Not all students of missions agree with the church growth reformers (any more than all their fellow churchmen agreed with Luther and Calvin), but all serious believers in the world-wide mission of the church are being vitally affected by the unrelenting call of church growth men to return to the Bible for the motive, the primary methods, and the standards for effecting Christian missions.

The return to the Biblical record makes one fact very clear: the modern missionary cannot be found in the early church. The early church did not practice "missions" as we do today. It possessed apostles, prophets, evangelists, pastors, teachers, miracle workers, healers, helpers, administrators, speakers in tongues, but not missionaries. The vast missionary enterprise of the nineteenth and twentieth centuries is not a direct descendant of first-century growth methods, but is a product of nearly two thousand years of Christian expansion. Some of the later additions to the missions effort should be kept; other additions have proved to be obstacles to effective church expansion. They must go.

The purpose of the chapters in Part I is to trace briefly the growth of missions as a separate activity of the church. From the early days of spontaneous expansion to the complex organizational structures of the nineteenth and twentieth centuries, dedicated Christians have reached out to the "lost and dying" peoples of the world to introduce them to the saving knowledge of Jesus Christ. The first chapter retells the story of that impulse to share the good news. Each unit highlights the particular contribution to church growth made during the chronological period under study. No attempt is made to introduce a "history of missions." These histories can be readily studied elsewhere.

The second chapter introduces the emphases of the church growth movement and its attempts to correct the mistakes of a missionary endeavor grown large, institutionalized, and sometimes self-serving. Fully appreciating the committed Christian persons who have given their lives in the cause of missions, church growth leaders nonetheless call for a reappraisal of traditional missionary approaches in the light of Biblical precedent and modern scientific methodology.

Chapter 1

CHURCH GROWTH AND TRADITIONAL MISSIONS

In his monumental study of the growth of the church, famed church historian Kenneth Scott Latourette[1] has identified four major periods of expansion. Each of these periods is characterized by new methods which revitalized the church. Each contributed to the development of mission outreach.

The first period of expansion lasted approximately five centuries, from the founding of the church until it was solidly established as the official religion of the crumbling Roman Empire. In the early days of this period the church grew by spontaneous expansion, but following Constantine's appropriation of Christianity as his official religion, it grew not so much through individual witnessing as through political edict and the conquest of new peoples through war.

The second era lasted from A.D. 950 to A.D. 1350 and witnessed the growth of the great monastic orders of Roman Catholicism.

The third period, encompassing the Protestant Reformation and the Roman Catholic Counter-Reformation, began in A.D. 1500 and ended in A.D. 1750. The primary methods for growth in this period were a continuation of those which characterized the previous ones. In this era Christianity gained a prominence and influence in human affairs that it had never had before. It expanded primarily through the exploration and colonization of the new world.

The final great period of events reached from 1815 to 1914 with Christianity's becoming truly a world religion by the latter date. In this century the great missionary societies of Protestantism and the denominational missions were born and flourished. We still live in the shadow of the great nineteenth century, so a completely objective analysis may not be possible for us. It is not too early to predict, however, that the decades will see substantial changes in mission patterns as a result of the work of church growth thinkers.

The following units will trace the growth of the church according to Latourette's categories. The reader is reminded that these units are only suggestive, not thorough, introductions to the contribution made by each era to the growth of the church's missionary outreach.

1: SPONTANEOUS EXPANSION

The growth of the church in its earliest centuries was little less than amazing. Who could have predicted that a fellowship which began with a few humble men could have just three centuries later exploded to become the official religion of the Roman Empire?

It was, furthermore, a "spontaneous expansion," to borrow Roland Allen's term, one "which follows the unexhorted and unorganized activity of individual members of the church explaining to others the Gospel which they have found for themselves."[2] No special persons were called missionaries. The church simply assumed that every Christian was a witness to his faith and that his faith would accompany him wherever he went. And those early Christians went. In fact, Stephen Neill writes, "nothing about the early Christians is more striking than the extent to which they managed to get about the world."[3] The apostle Paul set the example in church planting, but he was not alone. Hundreds of Christians carried the gospel around the known world, leaving behind young congregations of believers.

The simplicity of their approach should not be taken to indicate naiveté on the part of the believers nor a wholesale readiness on the part of the prospective converts, however. The church grew for several reasons: a burning belief in the lordship of Jesus Christ and a personal experience of His redeeming grace; a power

---

SPONTANEOUS VS. CONTROLLED EXPANSION

The Church of those ages was afraid of the human speculation of the learned men: we are afraid of the ignorance of illiterate men. The Church then maintained the doctrine against men who were consciously innovating: we maintain the doctrine against men who may unconsciously misrepresent the Truth that they have learnt. The Church then maintained the doctrine by her faith in it: we maintain our doctrine by distrusting our converts' capacity to receive it. The Church then maintained her doctrine by thinking it so clear that any one could understand it: we maintain our doctrine by treating it as so complicated that only theologians can understand it. Consequently, the Church then was quite prepared that any man who believed in Christ should teach others what he knew of Him: we are only prepared to allow men who have specially trained to teach it. When others, whom we have not specially trained, of their own spontaneous motion do teach others, we hasten to send a trained teacher to take their

---

16

place. That is, of course, exactly what the early Church did not do, yet it maintained its standard of doctrine.[4]

—Roland Allen
*The Spontaneous Expansion
of the Church*

* * * * *

Allen's remarks need to be compared, undoubtedly, with K.S. Latourette's more balanced analysis.

It is probable, however, that for about the first two centuries types of Christians existed one of whose chief functions it was to propagate the faith. It is clear that the authors of the Gospel of Matthew and the Acts of the Apostles believed that the Eleven were especially commissioned to proclaim the Christian message.[5]

It would propably be a misconception to think of every Christian of the first three hundred years after Christ as aggressively seeking converts. Such pictures as we have of these early communities in the New Testament and in the voluminous writings of these centuries warrant no such conclusion. In none of them does any hint occur that the rank and file of Christians regarded it as even a minor part of their duty to communicate their faith to others. It seems probable, however, that many incidentally have talked of their reli-

from the Holy Spirit in whom they trusted implicitly; an acquaintance with the cultures of those whom they witnessed; a common language; a sense of urgency to accomplish their task before the Lord returned; a willingness to challenge any adversary in the name of the Lord Jesus.

What strikes a twentieth-century reader of this early church history as strange, however, is the relative absence in the Scriptures and in the writings of the early church fathers of references to conversion or missions. Mission activity was not something separate from normal Christian witnessing. Since there was no specialized office of "missionary," each Christian carried the burden of witnessing to his faith. Furthermore, men like Tertullian believed that the Christian faith had already permeated every class of society by his time. The church had, in fact, they believed, expanded throughout the world.

gion to those whom they met in the round of their daily occupations.[6]
—Kenneth Scott Latourette
The First Five Centuries

* * * * *

That Christianity grew during these early centuries is obvious. What is not so obvious is why it flourished. The following sentences from Latourette's study of the history of Christian missions suggests the sources of Christianity's expansion:

1. *The endorsement of Constantine.* It was no minor cause of the part that Christianity was later to play in the world that the Church obtained the active endorsement of the head of the most powerful state of the time and that the particular monarch who initiated the policy stood out as among the ablest of the imperial succession and enjoyed a sufficiently long tenure of office to place the Church firmly in its new position.

2. *Disintegration of society.* The disintegration of existing cultures had become especially marked in the hundred and thirty years between Marcus Aurelius and Constantine. The disasters of these decades had weakened the established order, had made it less able to resist the inroads of a new faith, and had started many men on a quest for the sort of security which an authoritative religion seemed to offer.

3. *Organization which the Church developed.* No one of its rivals possessed so powerful and coherent a structure as did the Church. No other gave to adherents quite the same feeling of coming into a closely knit community.

4. *The Church's inclusiveness.* More than any of its competitors it attracted all races and classes.

5. *The Church's intransigence and flexibility.* In its refusal to compromise with the current paganism and with many of the social customs and moral practices of the times it developed a coherence and an organization which set it over against society. The very break required to join it gave to its adherents a conviction which constituted a source of strength against persecution and of zeal in winning converts.

6. *Christianity's religious and philosophical superiority.* Christianity supplied what the Graeco-Roman world was asking of religion and philosophy, and did it better than any of its competitors. As we have seen, the ancient world, and especially those portions of it in which Hellenistic influence was strong, believed in the distinction between matter and spirit. The former it regarded as evil and the latter as good. For it salvation meant the emancipation of the soul from the thraldom of matter and immortality through union with God. This was the object of the mysteries, of gnosticism, and of Neoplatonism. That salvation Christianity supplied. It had in the cross and the resurrection a dramatization of redemption which resembled the myths around which the mysteries were built. The Christians were convinced that they were heirs of a joyous immortality and in this assurance lay no small part of their appeal.

7. *Its Jewish origin.* The Hebrew Scriptures supplied the sanctity of a long development and the authority of antiquity. Then, too, in Hellenistic Judaism, Christianity found communities prepared for its message.

8. *Miracles.* Christianity was by no means the only cult which could claim the endorsement of the miraculous, but people looked to it to do for them what they expected of other religions and were not disappointed. To the Graeco-Roman world the existence of demons was almost as axiomatic as molecules, atoms, electrons, and germs have been to those reared in the science of the twentieth century. Christians claimed the power to expel evil spirits and could cite many instances of their success. The physical cures wrought by Christianity were among its claims for consideration.

9. *Moral qualities.* It was not merely that high ethical standards were held up before an age in which many were seeking moral improvement. Numbers of Christians found as well the power to forsake evil and approximate to those standards.

10. *Uniqueness of Jesus.* The more one examines into the various factors which seem to account for the extraordinary victory of Christianity the more one is driven to search for a cause which underlies them . . . It is *the uniqueness of Jesus* which seems the one tenable explanation of the fact that Christianity is the only one of the many Jewish sects to break off from the parent stem and outstrip it in size and influence. In the impulse which came from Jesus is the primary reason for that growth and that strength which attracted Constantine, for that vitality which enabled Christianity, in the keen competition among religions, to emerge the victor, and for the vision of a fellowship of disciples which led to its organization.[7]

★ ★ ★ ★ ★

1. Why shouldn't New Testament Christians simply return to New Testament missionary practices? Isn't it possible for modern missionaries to imitate the apostle Paul and adopt no other guide?

2. Since the word "missionary" is not to be found in the New Testament, are we justified in having missionaries today?

3. If it is true that today's missionary enterprise "is a product of two thousand years of expansion," of what value is it to seek New Testament precedents for today's missions?

4. Compare Latourette's analysis of early church growth with your own analysis of today's factors influencing church growth. What cultural factors are in our favor? What are not?

2: EXPANSION THROUGH POLITICAL POWER

After the Emperor Constantine adopted Christianity as his empire's official religion, the nature of the church and of its mission changed. Since all citizens of the empire were now nominal members of the Christian church, Christians thought less in personal and more in geographical terms about the expansion of the church. With the growth of the official church hierarchy, a gulf grew between clergy and laity. Order replaced spontaneity and specialized ministries replaced the priesthood of all believers. The church, newly married to the state, now had the authority to command obedience and conversion.

From the early days of Constantine's reign until the *de facto* separation of church from state authority, conquered peoples were regularly forced to bow before the cross and submit to Christian baptism as a sign of their submission to their conqueror. It was a violent age, and violence was used even in conversion. The penalties for violating some Christian rules in the days of Charlemagne (who ruled from 771 to 814) were severe in the extreme:

Anyone who kills a bishop, a priest, or a deacon, shall be put to death.

Anyone who burns the body of a dead person, as in the pagan fashion, shall be put to death.

Any unbaptized Saxon who attempts to hide himself among his own people and refuses to accept baptism shall be put to death.[8]

Centuries later, when Prussia was added to Christendom, one of the treaties ruled that

all who were not baptized must receive the rite within a month, that those who declined to comply should be banished from the company of Christians, that any who relapsed into paganism should be reduced to slavery, that pagan worship was to cease, that such Christian practices as monogamy were to be adopted, that churches were to be built, that the neophytes must attend church on Sundays and feast days, that provision must be made for the support of the clergy, and that the converts must observe the Lenten fast, make their confessions to a priest at least once a year, and partake of the Communion at Easter.[9]

It is obvious from the above that the church and the state were united in more than politics: they were in agreement in methods for dealing with those who did not submit to their authority. In fairness, however, we must add that whereas the conquering rulers often forced mass conversion upon the conquered foes, the church then assumed responsibility for the converts, nurturing them in the faith.

Missionaries, usually monks, attempted to teach at least the rudiments of doctrine to the new, still pagan members of the church.

* * * * *

1. During most of the history of Christendom, millions of converts have been added by compulsion. A victorious Christian people forced baptism upon the enemy. Although deploring the use of force, church growth leaders see real advantages in conversions *in mass.* What are these advantages? What are the dangers in such "mass movements"?

2. Most Americans are committed to the separation of church and state. This is, however, historically a very young concept. What was the relationship of religion and state in New Testament times? After Constantine? In America today?

3. Why have most rulers desired a united religion for their people?

3: EXPANSION THROUGH MONASTIC ORDERS

THE MONK AS MISSIONARY

The missionary function was originally not a primary aim of monasticism. Monks had, supposedly, separated themselves from society to achieve the salvation of their own souls and not for the purpose of helping others. Many, perhaps the majority of monks, held to this purpose and had little or no interest in the peoples outside their cells. However, some monks almost inevitably became missionaries. The monastic movement attracted those who were not content with the superficial religion which went by the name of Christianity, but were resolved to give themselves entirely to the faith. What more natural than that some of them should be caught by that desire to propagate the faith which from the beginning has been so integral a part of the genius of Christianity? Many, moreover, in search of solitude, pressed out beyond the borders of the society in which they had been reared, and built cells in the neighbourhoods where the only other inhabitants were non-Christians. Numbers acquired reputations for sanctity which attracted visitors and these contacts led to conversions. Some went out deliberately as missionaries. Then, too, the monastic congregation often proved an admirable missionary agency. Its fellowship strengthened the purpose of its members. In the West the prevailing Benedictine rule and the various reforming movements which arose out of it, like the Cistercians, stressed the importance of labour. In many a nominally converted region monks established themselves in fresh communities which cleared the forests, drained the swamps, introduced some of the arts of civilization, and gave religious instruction to the people about them. Yet the process of conversion and of raising the level of Christian living of the many neophytes of the mass movements might have proceeded more rapidly had missions been the primary monastic

With the marriage of church and state, the church by and large relaxed into comfortable conformity. The clergy became wealthy, the laity became dependent. But not entirely. Resisting the tempting allurements of a quasi-pagan society, many pious Christians advocated a separated life. These ascetics vowed to practice poverty and chastity and to live together in a separated, disciplined, monastic life. Many of these monks and nuns became missionaries to the frontiers of Rome's far-flung borders. It was, for example, a monk named Augustine whom Pope Gregory the Great sent to the British Isles in 596. Boniface, St. Patrick, St. Francis of Assisi—to name the great missionaries of the Middle Ages is to recognize our indebtedness to the monastic movement of the period.

Most of the early monastic houses were located in rural regions. The monks were farmers as well as devotees. Instead of threatening the folk ways in their communities, these sensitive Christians introduced their faith to their neighbors and appropriated native sacred festivals and places into the Christian year. Even those missionaries who had not read Pope Gregory's letter of July 18, 601, accommodated the faith to the people according to his instructions:

The heathen temples of these people need not be destroyed, only the idols which are to be found in them . . . If the temples are well built, it is a good idea to detach them from the service of the devil, and to adapt them for the worship of the true God . . . And since the people are accustomed, when they assemble for sacrifice, to kill many oxen in sacrifice to the devils, it seems reasonable to appoint a festival for the people by way of exchange. The people must learn to slay their cattle not in honour of the devil, but in honour of God and for their own food; when they have eaten and are full, then they must render thanks to the giver of all good things. If we allow them these outward joys, they are more likely to find their way to the true inner joy . . . It is doubtless impossible to cut off all abuses at once from rough hearts, just as the man who sets out to climb a high mountain does not advance by leaps and bounds, but goes upward step by step and pace by pace.[11]

—Pope Gregory

Church history of the Middle Ages testifies that Pope Gregory's instructions were faithfully obeyed—sometimes to the extreme. Numerous examples could be cited of the loss of identity which the church suffered in accommodating itself to the folkways of a region. More often, however, the church was successful in maintaining its uniqueness and transforming pagan practices into customs inspired with Christian meaning. Theologians and historians will long debate the effect of the church's determination to use the local language and local customs in order to present the universal Christ.

* * * * *

1. What resemblances do you note between the work of these medieval monks and that of modern missionaries?

2. What dangers do you see inherent in Pope Gregory's letter?

3. Latourette found the monastery tending "to remain somewhat aloof from the world" and pursuing "a self-contained routine." What safeguard against this fault does he suggest?

4: PROTESTANT MISSIONARY SOCIETIES

Protestant missions lagged so far behind Roman Catholic efforts that they undoubtedly deserved the taunts of the latter that Protestant churches were parochial, selfish, and unconcerned about the lost heathen of the world. Between 1500 and 1700 the aggressive Roman Catholics converted more people to Christ than they lost to the fledgling reform effort. Of course there were reasons for the Protestant tardiness. Herbert Kane gives these reasons,[12] summarized here.

Probably the most powerful reason was reformation theology, which taught that the Great Commission was only for the original apostles, who fulfilled it. Add to this the strong force of predestinarianism, which believed so strongly in the sovereignty of God that it held God totally responsible for saving the lost. Calvin summarized this position: "We are taught that the kingdom of Christ is neither to be advanced nor maintained by the industry of men, but this is the work of God alone." The Protestants were also anticipating an early end to the world, so a full-scale effort to reach the lost was deemed unnecessary. There was not sufficient time.

The second reason was the pitiful condition of the Protestant churches in this period. They were small, weak, and divided. Survival, not expansion, was their concern.

The third reason was their isolation. The Protestant lands, unlike Catholic Spain and Portugal, were not early colonial powers; they knew little of the so-called heathen lands.

Fourth, the Protestants did not enjoy the blessing of religious orders, whose dedicated celibates were unencumbered by family obligations and whose disciplined forces were ready to follow their church's commands to go withersoever. Protestant leaders encouraged family life, to the detriment of their evangelistic outreach.

In time, however, Protestantism experienced an outbreak of pietism similar to Roman Catholicism's ascetic movement of a millennium earlier. As those ascetics renounced all worldliness and advocated a holy life, the pietistic movement fathered by Philip Spener (1655-1705) encouraged prayer, Bible study, fellowship, and personal piety instead of the dogmatic legalism and civil war which had characterized Protestantism. In this atmosphere a new concern for spreading the gospel took root. Societies were formed in England, Europe, and North America between 1787 and 1815 in order to recruit, direct, and support missionaries. The new societies functioned like the orders of Roman Catholicism. The new missionaries became the elite of Protestantism. The theory of the priesthood of all believers, so idealistic a goal and so impractical in its results, gave way to the more pragmatic specialization of work and workers.

* * * * *

1. Why is it fair to assert that the missionary impulse originates in a believer's theology?

2. Why do Protestant Christians no longer agree with the Reformation understanding of the Great Commission?

3. In what ways is the mission of the church the work of God? In what ways is it the work of men and women?

5: NINETEENTH-CENTURY EXPLOSION

Nineteenth-century missions were dominated by powerful, spirited missionaries. Every school child knows the names of David Livingstone, Robert Moffatt, William Carey. Twentieth-century missions are still building upon the foundations laid by these pioneers. Their methods were as diverse as their personalities. Obeying the Great Commission meant translating the Bible; forming Sunday schools, English classes, sewing and homemaking classes; staffing medical clinics and educational institutions; assisting in agriculture, sanitation, governmental policies—and countless other activities. The Middle Ages had turned to the monastery for carrying the good news to the unevangelized. The nineteenth century replaced the monastery with the mission station, the monks with powerfully individualistic pioneers.

In addition to the strong personalities, nineteenth-century missions are characterized by the growth of mission societies. The men and the societies are intertwined. To mention William Carey, the "father of modern missions," for example, brings to mind the formation of the Baptist Missionary Society. In 1792 Carey published *An Enquiry Into the Obligation of Christians to Use Means for the Conversion of the Heathen* which, along with his sermon to a group of Baptist ministers at Nottingham on May 31, 1792, (in which he stated his two famous principles: "Attempt great things for God; expect great things from God") inspired the formation of the Baptist Missionary Society which sent him and his family in June, 1793, as the society's first missionaries. Missionary and society advanced together.

> ### WILLIAM CAREY AND CHURCH GROWTH
>
> Cary was extraordinarily independent and modern in his outlook. He saw missionary work as a five-pronged advance, with equal attention directed to each of the five elements: (1) the wide-spread preaching of the Gospel by every possible method; (2) the support of the preaching by the distribution of the Bible in the languages of the country; (3) the establishment at earliest possible moment of a Church; (4) a profound study of the background and thought of the non-Christian peoples; (5) the training at the earliest possible moment of an indigenous ministry.[14]
> —Stephen Neill
> *A History of Christian Missions*

James Hudson Taylor is another example. The Chinese Evangelization Society sent him to China in 1853, but that body failed to sustain him. The intrepid Taylor remained in China seven years, learning the language, journeying throughout the country—and finally resigning from the Society to depend on God alone. (His most controversial act during this period was the adoption of Chinese dress in an attempt to identify thoroughly with the Chinese people.) After returning to England in 1860 in ill health, Taylor founded the China Inland Mission, which became for awhile the largest mission in the world. Taylor realized that cooperation in mission was essential for church growth. He therefore adopted several unorthodox principles, many of them prophetic:[13]

1. The mission was to be interdenominational.
2. A door was opened for those with little formal education.
3. The direction of the mission would be in China, not in England.
4. Missionaries would wear Chinese dress, and as far as possible identify themselves with the Chinese people.
5. The primary aim of the mission was always to be wide-spread evangelism.

That his principles are a reaction to the prevailing practices of his time is evident. They stood for open fellowship among Christians of all conservative theological persuasions, against the growing proffessionalism of missionaries, against the dictatorial power of home-based boards and for the personal authority of the director on the field, for sympathy for the culture of the nationals, and against an overemphasis upon the shepherding of national Christians at the expense of converting the heathen. His obstacles were huge, but his successes were even greater, as recruits offered themselves in large numbers. By 1882 all the Chinese provinces had been visited and all but three boasted resident missionaries.

> Cary and Taylor were but two of the pioneering individuals who thought deeply about their evangelistic task. Twentieth-century missiologists are indebted to their experiments in relating the gospel to other nations. Evaluate Carey's insistence upon language study and Taylor's upon adopting native dress. How important are these?

Other stories could be told of the growth of mission societies in this great century, but they are amply narrated in mission histories.

The point is that the new spiritual vitality of pietism in Europe and North America gave birth to dozens of these societies between 1787 and 1914. The societies were organized to fill a void left by organized denominations. The world was rapidly expanding through trade, travel, and colonialism. The established churches were not equipped to evangelize the newly discovered areas. The societies accepted the challenge. In many ways these societies functioned like the various monastic orders of Roman Catholicism in the Middle Ages. Through their dedicated efforts Christianity grew rapidly on foreign soil.

A difference should be noted, however. The individualism of this robust period is seen in the relative lack of emphasis upon the church. Individual conversions, not the planting of churches, were the goal. In fact, in no period of church history have missionaries paid so little attention to building the church. Their goal was personal evangelism, not church planting.

Very often their nurturing efforts seemed to have little connection with their evangelizing and a great deal to do with "civilizing." They were so convinced of the superiority of their own cultures that they could not separate the gospel from culture. Alexander Duff, for example, the great Scottish missionary to India, was once asked why he was teaching English, philosophy, and science classes, instead of preaching the gospel. He replied simply that he was "laying a mine which in due course would explode and blow up the whole of Hinduism."[15]

> MONKS AND MISSIONARIES
> No doubt this position of being a class apart from all others has some advantages. Missionary groups are not unlike medieval monastic groups. As the monastics lived a life apart from the general body of Christians, and devoted themselves to the care of the sick, the ignorant, and the downtrodden, so do these; as the monastics devoted themselves to study and the production of Christian literature, so do these; as the monastics devoted themselves to a peculiarly religious life, so these missionaries represent the life of religion in a special sense, and certain peculiar outward piety is expected of them by those who are outside, even when they deride it. As monastics might be doctors, or teachers, or farmers, or traders, or students, or statesmen, but never belonged to any of these professions as they existed outside the monastic orders, so the missionary body embraces all these while yet it separates them by a subtle and invisible gulf from their fellow labourers in the same work outside. And as membership of a monastic group had certain advantages, so has membership of the missionary group; and as the monastic groups did great service to the church and to the state, so do these missionary groups.[16]
> —Roland Allen
> *The Ministry of the Spirit*

Finally, in 1961, in New Delhi, India, the World Council of Churches and the International Missionary Conference merged, with the WCC as the dominant body. Organizational unity of a kind had been achieved, but the theological issues which had troubled missionary thinking for most of the century remained unresolved: What is the church? What is mission? How should the Christian faith relate to non-Christian ones? What is the basis of authority? These and other such questions were ignored in the interest of ecumenical harmony.

In the growing theological confusion one fact became evident: the evangelizing of the nations was suffering. Traditional missionary societies began a systematic curtailment of evangelism in the Third World, leaving to the struggling young churches the responsibility for winning their own nations.

As the twentieth-century drift toward liberalism and stagnation became more evident, reaction by conservative Christians was inevitable. In 1955 the inevitable happened and the church growth movement was born.

For the history of the church growth movement refer to the Appendix.

Chapter 2
CHURCH GROWTH EMPHASES

The preceding chapter illustrates the evolving nature of the Christian mission. Each major era of Christian history contributed something new to the evangelistic outreach of the church. Church growth thinking does not repudiate this history; rather, it seeks to build upon the lessons which history teaches.

As a result of historical studies and observation of the contemporary mission scene, church growth leaders stress five fundamental emphases. No single church growth emphasis is peculiar to this school of mission thought, but church growth is unique in insisting upon all five as essential to a successful modern mission thrust.

Beginning with the primacy of a Biblical basis for mission, this chapter explores these fundamentals: evangelism as opposed to "good work" or "social action"; an optimistic, rather than a discouraged, attitude toward the gospel's opportunities in the world; scientific objectivity in the study of growth possibilities in place of the more traditional theoretical speculation which has prevailed in missiology; and the publishing of research undertaken to find how churches grow.

Insistence upon these emphases has provided church growth thought with a balanced, disciplined standard with which to study and judge mission effectiveness throughout the world. A grasp of this standard will enable missionary, churchman, and student to see mission as something other than simply doing a good work for the Lord. It will also reveal that obeying the Great Commission demands commitment of heart, soul, *and* mind. We go—not only sacrificially—but intelligently to proclaim the good news of Jesus Christ.

7: EMPHASIS ON THE BIBLE

But if we are to proclaim the gospel, we must understand it; if we are to baptize, we have to be persuaded that baptism is essential; if we are to plant churches, we need at least a minimum of dogmas. In short, I wonder whether one reason for the "partisan emphasis on peripheral aspects of the task," to which Dr. McGavran refers, may not be the theological context in which we are living. Statistics would probably show that missionaries in the typical mold, those namely who have clung to a concept of mission close to McGavran's own, are mainly recruited from pietistic, fundamentalist societies or circles, which are almost completely proof against the great currents of uncertainty in our time. In other words, the "McGavran strategy" can only be accepted and implemented by those with simple faith. I have no doubt that such faith can still move mountains. I fear that it is no longer within the reach of many Christians today.[1]

—Mme. E. Gouzée

A simple, fundamental, theologically unsophisticated faith—such is indeed an apt description of the basis of church growth's understanding of mission. This basis is no longer within reach of those who have rejected Biblical authority or who have lost the meaning of Jesus Christ as Savior and Lord—the only name by which men might be saved. Nor is it possible for those who blush at the church's attempts to "proselyte" believers from other religions. The Biblical view of the church, as Emil Brunner reminds us, is that "mission work does not arise from any arrogance in the Christian Church; mission is its cause and its life. The Church exists by mission, just as fire exists by burning. Where there is no mission, there is no Church, and where there is neither Church nor mission, there is no faith."[2] Faith leads to church; church leads to mission.

* * * * *

1. Do you agree with Mme. E. Gouzée that only those with a "simple faith" can accept the "McGavran strategy"? Defend your answer.

2. Have most Christians "outgrown" the theology which motivates church growth thinking?

3. Just what does theological growth mean, anyway?

Church growth theology accepts the authority of the Scriptures in all matters pertaining to faith and order for the individual Christian and for the church. If the Scriptures are not the authority, then what is? Recognizing that cultures vary from age to age and place to place, this stance nonetheless contends that the mission of the church remains unchanged until the close of history. Cultures vary, but the Word of the Lord remains constant, offering the words of salvation to all men everywhere.

Church growth theology is summarized simply in the two following statements.

A. Church Growth Theology is based on the fundamental principle that Scripture alone is the only infallible rule of faith and practice. The biblical record and interpretation of redemptive history is alone normative for mankind. There is no other Word of God. Inspired prophets interpreted to Old Testament Israel God's covenant with Abraham and his seed and spoke in various ways of the fact that all nations would be blessed through him. Inspired apostles interpreted to the New Testment Church the death, burial and resurrection of Jesus Christ, whereby He became Himself the blessing of the Abrahamic covenant—good news for all mankind. The acts and words of God in both testaments are foundational. Had they not occurred there would have been no normative interpretation, no scripture, no Church Growth Theology.[3]

B. Thus St. Paul seems to have left his newly-founded churches with a simple system of Gospel teaching, two sacraments, a tradition of the main facts of the death and resurrection, and the Old Testament. There was apparently no form of service, except of course the form of the sacraments, nor any form of prayer, unless indeed he taught the Lord's Prayer. There is no certain evidence of the existence of a written gospel or of a formal creed. This seems to us remarkable little. We can hardly believe that a church could be founded on so slight a basis. And yet it is possible that it was precisely the simplicity and brevity of the teaching which constituted its strength.[4]

It is obvious that the church did not conceive its purpose to be educational or medical. It felt no compulsion to attack the social evils of its day as its primary program. It did not attempt dialogue with any of the numerous established faiths of its time. It did not proclaim a new man come of age. If anything, the church emphasized the chasm of belief which separated itself from its pagan surroundings: to become a Christian was to turn from darkness into a marvelous light. Interestingly enough, it did not even worry about a modern emphasis in missions, strengthening the church. It assumed strength: it possessed the gospel, the living presence of the Holy Spirit, and all that was necessary for a full and abundant life here and eternal life hereafter.

* * * * *

CHURCH GROWTH AND THE WILL OF GOD

God wills the growth of His Church. A chief and irreplaceable element in her ministry is the proclamation of the Gospel to all mankind and incorporation of those who believe into her communal life. Only through the deliberate multiplications of vast numbers of new congregations all over the world will the Church be able to evangelize this generation. When she ceases to perform this mission, something fundamental is lost in her very essence as the people of God in the midst of the nations. The church that does not grow is out of the will of God.[5]

—Arthur F. Glasser

FOR FURTHER STUDY

The book of Acts is the first textbook on the growth of the church. Reread Luke's history of the early years of church expansion, paying particular attention to the factors which you think contributed to the growth of the church. You will want to note the influence of the following:

- strong, committed personalities
- leadership of the Holy Spirit
- importance and nature of preaching
- flexibility of strategy

In addition, answer the following questions:

Where did the apostle Paul go on his missionary journeys?

Who were the people who responded to the gospel?

What role did families play in the establishment of congregations?

What was the apostle's understanding of the church-as-institution?

What doctrine or traditions did the apostle deliver to the new churches?

What emphasis does the author of Acts place on numbers?

You will add several questions to this list. You will also want to read the epistles for further enlightenment on the nature of the early church.

* * * * *

1. Has our age become too complex and sophisticated to rely upon the Bible as the final authority for the church?

2. What is the authority for your personal faith?

3. What is the authority for your home church?

4. What is the purpose of God's revelation in the Old Testament and the New Testament? Has that purpose changed? How does the church assist God in His work?

5. How would you answer this question?

> If we are to have New Testament church growth today, flourishing in a New Testament climate, we too must be New Testament men. One asks immediately, "Do we want New Testament church growth in a New Testament climate?"
>
> I beg you not to answer Yes too quickly! Would we really feel at home in the New Testament church atmosphere, with miracles taking place around us, our deacons and leaders being martyred and our members run out of town?[6]

—Melvin L. Hodges

8: EMPHASIS ON EVANGELISM

What does the word *mission* mean? Having been applied too freely to such diverse activities as evangelism and industrial relations, it has come to mean everything and nothing. Bishop Neill reminds us: "If everything is mission, nothing is mission."[7] To some, mission is nothing less than God's total program for man. Practically, however, this definition means, as Bishop Neill warns, nothing. To church growth leaders, a more restricted, emphatic definition is needed: "We may define mission narrowly as *an enterprise devoted to proclaiming the Good News of Jesus Christ, and to persuading men to become His disciples and dependable members of His Church.*"[8]

Thus, as the following paragraphs indicate, church growth thinking maximizes evangelism and minimizes social action as the primary task of missions. When evangelism has been successful, churches will be planted, lives changed, and societies transformed, in that order.

Some may reply, "This talk of converting people offends us. It is proud and aggressive. The Christian should simply *be there,* quietly living as a Christian, worshiping as a Christian, meeting the issues of life as a Christian. Rather than seeking to aggrandize the Church and get people to join *his* church (a subtle form of ego inflation), he should simply pour himself out in quiet, kindly service and efforts to better the common lot of both pagans and Christians." To them, it must be said, "If quiet living as a Christian does in fact extend the faith and the Church, if under today's circumstances that mode of mission is *more effective,* there is no quarrel between you and us. But if quiet living is in fact denial of the universality of the Gospel, then your retreat into quietism should be branded for what it is—denial of the lordship of Christ."

The Pentecostal churches in Brazil and Chile, without calling their efforts industrial evangelism or trying to Christianize the framework of society, are doing much more of both than other churches in the world. *They are churches of the laboring masses.* Working men feel at home in them. Their leaders are thorny-handed men accustomed to wield hammer and pickax.

Pentecostals are multiplying churches in an apostolic fashion. One can reasonably expect that they will win a sufficient number of the proletariat to influence the course of civilization in Latin America. Changing the framework of society becomes increasingly possible as living churches multiply in Chile and Brazil. *This* is true industrial evangelism! It converts and transmits potency to the new Christians, who proceed promptly to bring other laboring men and women to potent, relevant Christian living.

Is there, then, no place for "concern for social justice" which attacks the evils in society just because men are God's children and their social structure should not deny them opportunity to live as such? Certainly there is a place! Christians should work to Christianize the social structure.

William Wilberforce, Toyohiko Kagawa, Frances Willard, and Martin Luther King have poured out their lives in highly desirable Christian activity. That is no reason, however, to confuse meaning and call their efforts evangelism. Christian social action is important in its own right. It does not need to take shelter under the prestigious word "evangelism."

Focusing attention on unsuccessful experiments, and carrying them on decade after decade, is a luxury which only wealthy churches and missionary societies can enjoy. When the source of income is assured and it makes little difference what is done so long as it has promotional value, then "missions" can indulge in all kinds of interesting and attractive ventures. If they wish to do so, they can enjoy themselves and call this "evangelism." These good ventures do not bring in churches which in turn extend the faith, upbuild the Church, and remake the framework of society in a more Christian world; but no matter—a splendid program of mission work is being carried on.

Poor churches, however, made up of Nazarenes, Wesleyans, and Pentecostals, by obedience (Acts 13:51; Mark 6:11; Matthew 10:14; Luke 9:5; 10:11), or by necessity, or by both, abandon unsuccessful experiments and hurry on to where men obey the Gospel gladly, are baptized, and form living, multiplying, society-changing churches.

Does concern for social justice convert? Well, does it? That is exactly the question.[9]   —Donald A. McGavran

Speaking against the modern emphasis on social service, Professor Kraemer writes:

To promise that Christianity will dispel economic misery and social disturbance is to invite inevitable disillusionment, because economic misery and social disturbance are caused and cured by many factors entirely outside the control of Church or missions. Sharing religious experiences, even service to men, "christianizing" the social, economic and political order, although necessarily included in the living act of manifold missionary expression, cannot be the real motive and ultimate purpose. The real motive and ultimate purpose are not founded in anything that men or civilizations or societies call for. As Kagawa has said, the starting-point of missions is the divine commission to proclaim the Lordship of Christ over all life; and therefore a return to the pristine enthusiasm for evangelism and a new vision of what this implies in word and deed in the present complicated world are needed.[10]

Hence McGavran:

> To put it simply and bluntly, when a Christian gives a cup of cold water because he is sure water is needed, and de-emphasizes conversion because he thinks Jesus Christ may not be the only gateway to eternal bliss, then his philanthropy is sub-Christian. Or again, for a disciple of Christ to promote amity between nations is good—if he does it knowing all nations live under the judgment of God and that amity is not their first need. But if his main *gospel* is solely that of good will between nations, then his promotion of amity is sub-Christian.[11]

* * * * *

The church growth school of thought has been charged with being unresponsive to the needs of the world for social justice, relief from poverty and oppression, for education and medicine. Its evangelistic emphasis is directed only at the souls and not at the bodies of men. From the beginning, however, church growth leaders have advocated a ministry to the total man.

> Teaching, preaching, and healing—inseparable in the ministry of Jesus—are projected in twentieth-century discipleship as school, church, and hospital. In presenting Christ to people who live in a predominantly non-Christian culture, where education and medical service have not been and are not otherwise available, these linked endeavors are most necessary. Where the church is at the center in a well-integrated service of preaching, teaching, and healing, the best results are obtained. The Christian who educates without imparting faith in the Christ or who heals the body without revealing Christ as Lord and Savior falls short in missionary obedience and betrays the Gospel.[12]
> —J. Waskom Pickett
> *The Dynamics of Church Growth*

Church growth leaders have also called for proportion in mission.

> It holds that men have multitudinous needs of body, mind and soul to meet which is thoroughly Christian. The Church is properly engaged in relief of suffering, pushing back the dark pall of ignorance, and increasing productivity. But such activities must be carried out in proportion. They must never be substituted for finding the lost. Christians must never be guilty of turning from the Spirit to the flesh or of deceiving men by offering them transient betterment as eternal salvation.

In regard to the battle raging today between advocates of evangelism and social service, we say that finding the lost and bringing them back to the Father's House is a chief and irreplaceable purpose of Christian mission. It is not the *only* purpose. It is not even *the* chief purpose. It is, however, *a chief and irreplaceable* purpose. Finding the lost is not simply "a chief purpose." That opens the door to very minor emphasis on what was a major emphasis in the New Testament Church. That allows men to slight our Lord's great commission. Bringing the lost home is a *chief and irreplaceable purpose.*[13]

—Donald McGavran

★ ★ ★ ★ ★

1. In your opinion, is evangelism the primary task of church's mission? What is the basis of your opinion?

2. How has your church in America been growing? What are the causes for its growth or lack of growth?

3. What do you consider to be the proper relationship of evangelism to social action?

9: EMPHASIS ON OPPORTUNITY

Church growth leaders are famous for their belief that this is "a most responsive world," one in which a "fantastic increase" in the number of Christians is both essential and possible. This optimism is based upon a firm belief that the "God Who Finds is now and always will be in charge of His mission. He intends today that His banquet hall be filled. If one group refuses, then another must be persuaded."[14] Admitting that many areas of the world are difficult for the Christian mission, church growth men encourage missionaries to turn their energies toward those lands or peoples whose receptivity is evident.

Why should we go?

In God's good purpose, many people today are ripe for the harvest. His evident intention is that white fields should be reaped. In this kind of a world God will constrain His servants to reap the harvest. The same Holy Spirit who inspires men to claim the world for Christ, also inspires them to concentrate their efforts on those areas where men are gladly coming to the Saviour.[15]

—Donald McGavran

Where should we go?

Searching for truth, no matter where it may lead us, we have been pressured by the weight of evidence into accepting the revolutionary idea that during these decades, the world is much more receptive to the Gospel than it has been in 1900 years. This idea is enhanced when mankind is viewed as a vast mosaic of ethnic, linguistic and cultural units. Citizens of India, for example, are not just Indians. They are members of several thousand ethnic units called castes. They are further divided by languages and dialects, and by educational and economic levels. Urban units are very different from rural units.

In almost every land some pieces of the mosaic are receptive to the Gospel. People after people, tribe after tribe, caste after caste, is now winnable. Urban segment after urban segment can now be discipled. After a professor in Hindustan Bible Institute, which enrolls 140 men training for the ministry, had studied at Fuller Seminary's School of Missions and after a Church Growth Seminar in Madras, the faculty of the Hindustan Bible Institute decided that it was feasible to plant 100 new congregations in Madras City in receptive units of that huge metropolis.

Again after Dr. E. C. Smith got his Master of Arts in Missiology at the Pasadena School and returned to Java, the Southern Baptist Mission there had an extraordinary spiritual revival, in the course of which it embarked on a deliberate policy of starting—to use its words—"thousands of house and hamlet churches" among the receptive Moslems and Chinese of East Java. The mission had started looking at East Java as a mosaic, some parts of which are receptive. It had discovered a degree of receptivity so large that only a goal such as the mission adopted would match the opportunity.

Three years ago, I often said that in Africa by the year 2000 there would be a hundred million Christians. Dr. David Barrett told me he thought my estimate far too conservative. I asked him to make one of his own and let me print it. He kindly proceeded to do the demographic calculation necessary and his estimate appeared in the May 1969 issue of the Church Growth Bulletin. He judged that by A.D. 2000 there would be 357 million Christians in Africa! Later, the *International Review of Missions* picked up the story and then *Time* and other newspapers broadcast it, and it has now (1972) become part of much Christian thinking.[16]

—Donald McGavran

When should we leave a field?

If then we go on teaching where that moral response is refused, we cease to preach the Gospel; we make the teaching a mere education of the intellect. This is why so much of our teaching of the Gospel in schools and zenanas is ineffective. We teach, but we do not teach morally. We do not demand moral response. We are afraid to take the responsibility which morally rests upon us of shaking the lap. We should refuse to give intellectual teaching to a pupil if he refused to give us his attention: we might equally refuse to give religious teaching to a pupil who refused to give us religious attention.

It is a question which needs serious consideration whether we ought to plant ourselves in a town or village and continue for years teaching people who deliberately refuse to give us a moral hearing. We persevere in this in spite of the fact that near at hand are men who are eager and willing to give us that moral hearing. We are afraid to take responsibility which morally rests upon us of shaking the lap. We have forgotten that the same Lord who gave us the command to go, gave the command to shake off the dust from our feet. We have lost the art of shaking the lap, we have learnt the art of steeling our hearts and shutting up the bowels of our compassion against those who cry to us for the Gospel.[17]

—Roland Allen

When can we quit?

When our Lord commands us to make disciples of the nations, He surely does not consider the job successfully concluded when one in 100 has yielded Him allegiance. Burying even 1 or 2 per cent in a napkin to return to Him after thirty years, still 1 or 2 per cent, will scarcely merit His "well done."

Nor can it be safely supposed that better living, a more Christian social order, The Kingdom of God on earth, a vast increase of brotherhood, justice, and peace can be obtained while only one in 100 is a church member. That would be impossible in Tennessee. Why blithely imagine it possible in Thailand?[18]

—Donald McGavran

Why hasn't there been more growth?

A. Paucity of knowledge concerning people movements, receptive populations, arrested Christian movements, the effects of revivals, the real outcome of the school approach in Africa, and a hundred other aspects of mission keeps the church-mission organism working in the dark, going it blind concerning its God-given task. All kinds of theories as to the desirability of methods (such as dialogue with non-Christian religions, industrial evangelism, and accommodation to culture) are propounded without adequate knowledge as to the effect these have on bringing ta ethne to faith and obedience.

Enough discipling is not happening—this is typical church growth thinking. Traditional missions take offence at the word "enough" and like to consider lack of discipling as inevitable in the view of the hardness of the world or the lack of funds. Church growth men recognize, of course, that some fields are so resistant that no Church grows; but they also recognize that often appeal to the difficulty of the field simply masks the fact that the Church concerned is not seeking lost sheep or is resolutely looking for them in ravines where they are not grazing. In Chile, for example, all the old line missions are getting very little growth in a country where several hundred thousand have become Evangelical Christians in Pentecostal Churches.[19]

—Donald McGavran

B. I do not think that we reflect sufficiently upon the fact that most of the fundamental forms of our churchmanship were laid down during a period in which Christianity was a contracting and not an expanding religion, the period in which, hemmed in by power of Islam and isolated from the great non-Christian cultures of the East, Christendom almost lost the consciousness of the world which was still waiting to be evangelized. Bishop Lancelot Andrewes, writing at the beginning of the seventeenth century when the evangelization of Asia, Africa and the Americas had scarcely yet been dreamed of among non-Roman Christians, could give thanks "for the more than marvellous conversion of all the world to the obedience of faith." Christendom had become a self-contained world; the sense that the Church is a body sent into all the world, a body on the move and existing for the sake of those beyond its own borders, no longer played an effective part in men's thinking. This fact is reflected in the fundamental forms of our church life. The ministry is conceived almost exclusively in pastoral terms as the care of souls already Christian. The congregation is seen as a body existing for the edification and sanctification of its own members rather than for witness and service to the world outside. Our very systems of doctrine tend to be constructed vis-a-vis other Christian systems, rather than vis-à-vis the great non-Christian systems of thought. And the normal content of a course in Church history has far more of the mutual disputes of Christians than of the missionary advances of the Church and the encounter of the gospel with the non-Christian cultures which it has successively met and mastered.[20]

—Lesslie Newbigin

This unit has asked several questions to focus the reader's attention on the amazing opportunities for discipling the nations today. Return now to the same questions with America in mind. Why should we go—in America—to the non-Christian? Where will we find him? When should we give up on him? When should we feel that we have fulfilled our responsibility to the Great Commission? Why hasn't there been more growth?

Many American Christian groups are growing rather phenomenally. Others are not. Why?

10: EMPHASIS ON SCIENTIFIC OBJECTIVITY

Heeding Donald McGavran's appeal to "switch to the strategy of the era now beginning" instead of continuing to use "the strategy of an era now closing,"[21] the church growth movement freely appropriates insights from every available theoretical and practical scientific discipline: from anthropology, sociology, linguistics, computer technology, communications technology. It is also sensitive to the lessons of history, literature, and other cultural disciplines. Its primary methodological concern is to break out of any theoretical prison into the freedom of facts. Hence case studies of actual situations are exhibits in the argument for church growth. Church growth studies do not try to impress academicians, but prod missionaries and mission executives into rethinking their own activities, for the studies show percentages of growth, causes for blocked growth, instances of "cultural overhang" on the part of missionaries, and suggested remedies.

Church growth's emphasis upon scientific methods is an insistence upon objectivity, a determination to study every mission situation without prejudice. Such objective study should enable missionaries to view their adopted countries with cultural appreciation, thus avoiding the confusion of Christianity with western civilization which adversely affected nineteenth- and early twentieth-century missions.

UNDERSTANDING THE CULTURE

The missionary . . . wishing to communicate the Gospel or a socio-economic idea must proceed not only from the known to the unknown but also from the felt to the still unfelt, from the wanted to the still unwanted. Above all, conviction and persuasion call for the use of effective, culturally pertinent "starting-points" of reasoning, feeling, and motivating, the so-called basic assumptions, emotionally charged attitudes, and goals that underlie all conviction and persuasion . . . Human beings, no matter how simple or how sophisticated, may indeed reason, react emotionally, and be moved to action according to the same psychological laws, but the underlying assumptions and drives will differ from culture to culture. A successful argument must be in harmony with such underlying assumptions and premises (for example, face-saving in the Orient) otherwise the best oratory and logic will fail. Persuasion is successful only if the motives be real, that is, real to the receiver of the message. This is the only effective procedure in intercultural communication, a procedure that presupposes a thorough acquaintance with the culture content and the particular value-system of the receiving society.[22]

—Louis J. Luzbetak
The Church and Cultures

* * * * *

1. What is the danger in confusing the standards of practices of culture with those of the Bible?

2. Isn't it an objective fact that Western civilization is superior to all others, especially those of the under-developed countries?

3. What are some of the presuppositions of American middle-class culture which might adversely affect the Christian mission in other countries?

4. What should church buildings look like?

5. What practices in your church are definitely commanded in the Bible and what are commanded by your culture?

11: EMPHASIS ON PUBLISHING

Church growth was born in research. From the 1935 study of mid-India's church growth to the latest statistics compiled by associates in church growth at the School of World Mission in Pasadena, leaders in the movement have been gathering data and sharing results with their colleagues around the world.

> Convinced that hundreds of millions who have yet to believe are diverted from knowing Christ through a paucity of knowledge concerning discipling, the Church Growth School of Thought lays great emphasis on scientific research to ascertain the factors which affect reconciling men to God in the Church of Jesus Christ. We believe that tremendous discoveries await us there. Where have denominations grown? Where have congregations multiplied? Where have they *not* grown? How much—or how little—have they grown? Above all, why have they grown? This last question may be asked in an exact way by saying "Why has each segment of the Church grown? We must know accurately the growth patterns characteristic of thousands of pieces of the mosaic.
>
> Church growth men believe that the hard facts about church growth once discovered should be published, taught to ministers and missionaries, read by serious minded Christians and used in all evangelistic labors whether in the local churches or in nations.
>
> We encourage those who write master's theses and doctor's dissertations to publish them. We believe that, far from withholding publication until a highly polished research has been done, it is desirable to publish "research in progress." We live in the midst of an explosion of information. Mission must discover more and more about its field and disseminate what it discovers. We hope our convictions on these matters will commend themselves to fellow professors of missions, mission executives and leaders of younger Churches and older Churches. A firm foundation of facts needs to be placed under the missionary enterprise. To do it, large scale cooperation among Christians of many lands and many cultures is urgently required.[23]
>
> —Donald McGavran

In the first issue of *Church Growth Bulletin*, McGavran insisted upon precision of language and reliance upon fact.

> Christian mission wanders in a rosy fog of vague objectives and promotional hopes. Its objectives are frequently phrased in words —outreach, extension of the Gospel, witness, opening a province, beginning a work, carrying on mission work—as vague as they are wide. "Outreach"—to what end? Beginning what kind of "work"? Instead of ambiguous and slippery terms, Christian mission needs to

speak positively and exactly about the growth of the Church. Not what missionaries did, but how churches grew. Not national trends, but how congregations arose. Not nationalization, urbanization, devolution and mechanization, but how well are we getting on with discipling a particular part of a particular nation? Not "what do they eat," but "have they confessed Christ"?[24]

Throughout the years since the establishing of the Institute of Church Growth in 1960, a team of researchers has joined McGavran in intensively asking "How do churches grow?" Anthropologists, sociologists, theologians, linguists; experts in the phenomenology of tribal religions, in education by extension, in cultural psychology, in the history of revivalism—and on could go the list of men and women who combine practical field experience with scientific discipline. As a result of their collaborative efforts, research projects have begun to form patterns which Peter Wagner calls "models for missiological research."

Research projects over the years have begun to form certain patterns which might be described as models for missiological research . . . Six general categories can be discerned at the present time.

1. *Church Growth Area Surveys.* These research projects give a general picture of the Church in an area of the world. The principal example of this kind of research is *Latin American Church Growth,* a book by William Read, Victor Monterroso and Harmon Johnson published by Eerdmans in 1969. It has subsequently been published in both Spanish and Portuguese and has been widely read by Christian Workers.

2. *Church Growth National Surveys.* These projects record the history of the Church in a given nation, attempting to interpret history in terms of the dynamics of growth and non-growth of the Churches. As do most SWM [School of World Mission, Fuller Theological Seminary] research projects, these end with a concluding section on "hard, bold plans for church growth." Published examples include Grimley and Robinson on Nigeria, Olsen on Sierra Leone, Wagner on Bolivia, Tuggy and Toliver on the Philippines, and Enns on Argentina.

3. *Church Growth Denominational Surveys.* These projects have been conducted on both international and national bases. They are perhaps the most popular type of research since they provide the student an opportunity to analyze the work with which he is most familiar and make projections for future strategy on the basis of his research. This has been exceedingly helpful to mission management

even though it has caused some dismay. When personalities and contemporary issues are involved, it is often difficult to strike a balance between courage and frankness on the one hand and discernment and tact on the other. Conrad's survey of Nazarene missions world-wide is an example of the international model. Nationally, Shearer on the Presbyterians in Korea and Kwast on the Baptists in West Cameroon are examples of what can be done.

4. *Analysis of Missionary Methodologies.* This type of study zeros in on a particular missionary method or the method of a particular society. It tests its effectiveness against the goals that have been set by workers using it, and makes suggestions for reinforcement or modification as the case may be. Some outstanding examples are Bradshaw on Evangelism-in-Depth, Voelkel on Latin American student work, Chua on Asian student work and Braun's significant book *Laity Mobilized.*

5. *Biblical and Theological Principles.* Interest in research in this area is growing in SWM. Murphy's thesis on Spiritual Gifts and Evans on Spirit Possession are examples of the application of church growth principles to theology and biblical studies. Research in progress in this field includes Professor Norvald Yri on The Principle of Religious Authority in the Norwegian Lutheran Church and the Faith and Order Movement; Dagfinn Solheim on the Theology of Missions in the Confessional Lutheran Tradition; Professor Edward Pentecost on The Theology of Missions in the Dispensational Tradition; and Pablo Perez on the Latin American theology.

6. *Elenctics or the Science of bringing peoples of non-Christian religiosity to repentance and faith.* Non-Christian religions become the subjects of research in order to be able to present convincingly to their devotees the claims of Christ. Examples of this kind of research include Gustafson on Thai Buddhism, Gates on Chinese Animism, Johnson on Brazilian Spiritism and Nordyke on Aymara Animism.

As time goes by, undoubtedly new models for missiological research will be added to this list. Every attempt is made to be flexible enough to allow each associate freedom in selecting an area of research that will meet his particular needs and be most helpful in his future work.[25]

The purpose of this research has been succinctly stated by McGavran:

We devise mission methods and policies in the light of what God has blessed—and what He has obviously not blessed. Industry calls this "modifying operation in light of feedback." Nothing hurts missions overseas so much as continuing methods, institutions, and policies which ought to bring men to Christ—but don't; which ought to multiply churches—but don't; which ought to improve society—but don't. We teach men to be ruthless in regard to method. If it does not work to the glory of God and the Extension of Christ's church, throw it away and get something which does. As to methods, we are fiercely pragmatic—doctrine is something entirely different.[26]

This research is, of course, not for the sake of research. It is goal-oriented, to be used by mission leaders everywhere who are making decisions that will affect the lives of millions of future Christians. Whenever possible, church growth leaders and students hasten the results of their studies into print. Several religious publishers have begun disseminating church growth books (most notably Eerdmans and Moody Press), and a new publisher, The William Carey Library, has been born for no other purpose.

★ ★ ★ ★ ★

1. Some critics could claim that church growth's emphasis upon research, using words like "feedback" and "pragmatic," sounds too much like American business and too little like God's business. Just how "business-like" or "scientific" or "scholarly" should the work of God become?

2. McGavran makes a sharp separation between method and doctrine. He is "ruthless" in method, but sees doctrine as something different. In what ways, however, is our method determined by our doctrine? For example, are there some things your doctrine of the church will not allow you to do in order to help the church to grow?

3. Church growth study to date has been almost exclusively related to Third World. Why has church growth study in America been so tardy in developing, in your opinion? How would you begin? What kinds of studies are needed?

4. Look at your home congregation. How much has it grown in the past decade? In what age groups? Among what socio-economic-racial classes? Through what programs? What changes would you recommend?

PART II

THE SCIENCES OF MAN AS AIDS
TO CHURCH GROWTH

Church growth men take the input of behavioral sciences seriously. While Christian theology informs them of the fundamental human predicament without God and of the gospel of salvation, behavioral sciences can provide them with insights into cultural, social, and psychological frames of reference in which the peoples of the world live. Convinced of the Biblical mandate to proclaim the gospel, church men appropriate the sciences of man as aids to further the expansion of Christ's church on earth. Chapter 3 gleans the insights from behavioral sciences applicable to church growth.

In attempting to execute the Great Commission faithfully, church growth men believe that research is the crucial link between devotion to ineffective evangelism and discovery of fruitful strategy. Since little is mentioned in available literature about the procedure of church growth research which can be applied to the American scene, Chapter 4 will explain this procedure.

Chapter 3
INSIGHTS FROM BEHAVIORAL SCIENCES

The academic disciplines of anthropology, psychology, and sociology are grouped together under the category of behavioral sciences. These sciences can offer many insights into the expansion of Christianity. They can inform the missionary about culture and behavior of the people to whom he is sent. The missionary, in his effort to present the gospel, must know the best way to communicate it within that culture. He needs to acquaint himself with the patterns of thinking and behaving prevalent among the people. These patterns are as different as the variety of social units and their sub-cultures even within one society. No two groups are receptive to the presentation of the gospel in exactly the same manner because of the differences in their socio-cultural backgrounds. Therefore, by first studying the people in their unique cultural context anthropologically, psychologically, and sociologically, a missionary can expect to present the message of redemption in such a way as to avoid cultural repercussions.

Unit 12 discusses the insights which anthropology can give to mission and church growth. The problem of polygamy is keenly felt on the missionary frontier and is dealt with in Unit 13 as an example of the application of anthropology to mission. Where the Scripture is silent on this particular problem, how are we to solve it? Anthropology does help clarify some knotty cultural issues surrounding the institution of polygamy in the process of making a decision. Unit 14 investigates the contribution which psychology can make to church growth studies. The subject of receptivity is explored, but the unit remains suggestive rather than conclusive concerning the contribution of psychology to church growth. Units 15—17 examine the relevance of sociology to church growth studies and the concepts of social structure and homogeneous units as they illumine the growth processes of the church.

12: ANTHROPOLOGY IN MISSION WORK

Some pertinent questions are raised and answered in this unit concerning the application of anthropology—more specifically, cultural anthropology—to mission and church growth. Before proceeding further, ask yourself the following questions:

1. Should anthropolgy be used to further church growth? For that matter, should any branch of science be utilized to accomplish what is commanded by God?

2. Does not the application of anthropology to missionary endeavor imply our lack of confidence in the work and power of the Holy Spirit? Does not the employment of techniques developed by scientific research as such imply the same?

3. How can anthropology help missionary endeavor? What specific insights can it offer to mission?

4. How do you define culture?

* * * * *

Should Anthropology Be Used to Further Church Growth?

The Christian missionary who believes that in Jesus Christ God has revealed a way of life rewarding for all men, also uses anthropology for directed change. He too is aware that it is impossible for various cultures to remain in their present state of development. Like other practitioners of applied anthropology, he is opposed to sacrificing the welfare of any people in order to keep it as a museum piece. He is opposed to leaving directed change in the hands of the exploiter, materialist, communist, blind chance, or selfish racism. He believes that God is calling the Church to play its part in bringing about a social order more in harmony with His will—more just, brotherly and peaceful. In becoming Christian, increasing numbers across the nations take the most important single step in directed change. This is the humane reason why the missionary is engaged in discipling the nations. The authority for discipling the nations, seen in the Bible, fits so extraordinarily well with what his reason tells him is essential for the maximum welfare of the maximum number of men.

The Christian then turns to anthropology with a good conscience to discover why certain churches have grown and others have not, and to devise customs, institutions and other configurations which fill the voids created by rapid social change, in a manner acceptable to the society in question.[1]   —Donald McGavran

Does Not the Application of Anthropology to Missionary Endeavor Imply Our Lack of Confidence in the Work and Power of the Holy Spirit?

In the first place, the very word "anthropology" still seems to cause some people to avoid all association with it. The connotation given it by such theories as human evolution as developed by the branch of physical anthropology makes the whole field suspect. However, even a cursory study of the field soon reveals that there is much more to anthropology than this aspect of physical anthropology: linguistics, archeology, and cultural anthropology are other branches (following American terminology). It is the latter branch, cultural anthropology, which is of particular interest to missionary anthropologists, since it is the science which studies all of man's learned behavior.

Right at this point a second basic misunderstanding takes place. Many do not take into consideration that different peoples have different systems of learned behavior. Not only can their language and religious expression be different, but their economic, social, and technological systems can also be extremely different. We are accustomed to communicating and dealing with people of our own cultural background, who have learned more or less the same system of behavior that we have. When we talk or preach to our own people, we take for granted that we are understood, because of our similar backgrounds. And yet, even in this case, we often speak of talking "on someone's level." Older people are notoriously known for their misunderstanding of the younger generation. Here, again, there is a difference in behavior from one age group to another even

> Culture is a design for living. It is a plan *according to which society adapts itself to its physical, social and ideational environment.* A plan for coping with the physical environment would include such matters as food production and all technological knowledge and skill. Political systems, kinship and family organization, and law are examples of social adaptation, a plan according to which one is to interact with his fellows. Man copes with his ideational environment through knowledge, art, magic, science, philosophy, and religion. Cultures are but different answers to essentially the same human problems.[2]
>
> —Louis J. Luzbetak
> *The Church and Cultures*

within a system that is shared to a large extent. To overcome these barriers, Christian workers (and anyone wishing to work at these age levels) take courses about children and their behavior; youth workers study the problems and psychology of teen-agers to be able to understand them and to communicate with them more effectively.

In the above examples, a conscious adjusting of the approach takes place on the basis of the knowledge acquired. To do so is not considered as limiting or having no regard for the role of the Holy Spirit. It is looked upon as common sense. . . .

How much more true is this in a cross-cultural situation, where the cultural systems and background of the foreign Christian worker and the local people are more radically different. It is precisely at this point that anthropology can help. The task of a missionary anthropologist is to bring to light the problems that exist, so that his understanding of the culture will be more complete, and that communication of the gospel can be more effective . . . the anthropologist simply helps to clear away the barriers to communication, so that the missionary can speak to his hearers and truly reach them. . . . When the message is received with understanding, then the Holy Spirit can work with the fullness of his power in the hearts of men. To the question of Romans 10:14—"And how are they to believe in him of whom they have never heard?"—might be added this corollary: And how are they to believe if they have never understood?[3]

—Harold W. Fehderau

What Are the Specific Insights
Which Anthropology Can Offer to Mission?

A word about the relevance of anthropology to the trends and movements in the missionary cause would perhaps be in order. That complex of attitude and behavior known as "paternalism" is badly out of fashion now, but what is replacing it? The answer often comes in terms of "equality," "fraternal relationship," "independence," "identification," etc. Much of this important current emphasis risks being a travesty if it is not based on profound mutual understanding between those who are in "fraternal relationship." One of the important roads to mutual understanding and respect is the insight which anthropology can offer.

Anthropology has a great deal to offer to the younger churches and to outsiders who try to work with the younger churches. It has much to offer to the contemporary emphasis on the church *in* society and the church *as* society. As churches seek, under God, to find solutions to the social problems of the culture in which they are growing, anthropology can help them to see these institutions or patterns of behavior more objectively. . . .

Anthropology offers specific techniques for learning about people and their culture. . . .

Anthropology offers source materials and analyses of specific societies in many parts of the world. For some groups of people the missionary can find numerous volumes of anthropological study. For others there is sketchy work, or none at all. Most important culture *areas* of the world, however, do have representative works which are most helpful because of resemblances between peoples within the area. . . .

Insight into the meaning of behavior is another important contribution of anthropology. People in different societies sometimes mean entirely different things by the same action. The thoughtful study of anthropology inevitably breeds a healthy degree of cultural relativism as an institution such as the "bride price" or subordinate status of women, or marriage arranged by parents, or a definition of incest which includes the father's brother's children, but not the father's sister's children, are seen in terms of their functional relevance within a society; and, on the other hand, some of our most cherished customs are seen to be the product of our own particular history. This kind of cultural relativism, a degree of freedom from ethnocentrism, is essential if we are not to insist on the automatic importation of our cultural God and the supercultural faith and love which He engenders in men on the basis of His revelation of himself to them in cultural form in the Scriptures and in the lives and words of His missionaries.

THE INDIVIDUALITY OF A CULTURE

One of the most common pitfalls in any cross-cultural activity is the tendency to lose sight of the uniqueness of cultures. Every design for living has, so to speak, a personality or individuality of its own. There is a rather general tendency in any observer of foreign ways to give identical interpretations to behavioral patterns whenever and wherever even superficial similarities are found. Identical usages, identical functions, and identical values are attributed to similar customs. Thus, although the high value placed on virginity in some parts of the world has an economic rather than a moral or religious basis, the unwary outsider, observing the high esteem of the people for bridal integrity, will admire them for their high moral standards when actually they should be praised for their good economic and purely materialistic sense—the bride-price happens to be much higher for a virgin than a non-virgin.[4]
—Louis J. Luzbetak
The Church and Cultures

Anthropology offers the value of seeing cultures as "wholes." Anthropology studies social structure in relation to economics, to religion, to technology, etc. Agriculture techniques are not enough in themselves, but they have a relation to the family structure of the people who performs them, to religious rites, to the yearly cycle of labor, etc. Above all, religion cannot be isolated from the remainder of life. The tendency to compartmentalize its religion, which is a characteristic of American culture, is not shared by most other societies in the world. Conversion, and resulting changes in behavior, will have far-reaching effects if they are at all profound. . . .[5]

—William A. Smalley

13: POLYGAMY AND CHURCH GROWTH

A Puzzle Raised by Polygamy

Kenneth Taylor relates his experience of conversing with a group of missionaries in Africa. The subject of conversation around the supper table was the chief of a nearby village who had recently become Christian. Mr. Taylor writes:

The missionaries had carefully instructed him about the Christian life as they had been taught it, and pointed out to him that the very first thing after disposing of idols or fetishes must be the disposing of all but one wife.

"Did you hear," asked one of the missionaries, "that the chief got rid of one of his wives last week?"

"No," replied the others, "how did it happen?"

"Well," said the first missionary, "it seems he has a brother who wanted another wife and he invited his brother to come and he lined up his wives and told his brother to take any one that he wanted and he could have her. So the brother took one of them with him."

> ### HOW DID POLYGAMOUS MARRIAGES GET STARTED?
>
> Social systems which permit polygamous marriages have been common throughout the earth. Continuously warring societies often killed off men rapidly. It became normal for polygamous households to arise. In some societies, having many wives meant more grain, larger sweet potato gardens, or more wives meant more success. In still other societies, chiefs effected political liaisons of various sorts through plural marriages. Many other situations led to polygamy being a normal and legitimate mode of marriage. The Mosaic Law specifically allowed polygamy and, in the case of a brother who died without issue, required it.[6]
>
> —Donald McGavran
> *Church Growth Bulletin*

"Well, praise the Lord!" another of the missionaries exclaimed. I'm afraid that I was lost in thought long after the supper table conversation ended. In my mind's eye I could see that poor woman, divorced by her husband, forced into a life of adultery with her husband's brother, taking her little children with her and being led off into the darkness of the heathen night out of the radiant light of the gospel, transformed out of the Kingdom of His dear Son back into the darkness controlled by the principalities and powers of heathenism. . . .

Somehow the exultant words of the missionary praising the Lord because the woman had been divorced and sent away turned bitter in my ears.[7]

—Kenneth N. Taylor
Eternity Magazine

The Crucial Issue Regarding Polygamy

As Christianity spread throughout Europe, however, its high valuation of women plus many other factors, including centuries when
Church and State were united, brought it about that Christians considered monogamy an essential part of Christianity. During the missionary movement of the last two centuries, when Christianity, the
religion of the great powers, was propagating itself among the peoples of Asia and Africa, many of which were polygamous, it took a
very strong stand against polygamy. Polygamists could not become
Christians. In order to be baptized, men had to give up all but one
wife. The prestige of Christianity in some places brought about
Christward movements with a radical renouncing of polygamy. In
other places, people stuck to polygamy and rejected Christianity. All
across Africa, the typical outcome was for peripheral persons
and school children to become Christians while the village power
structure—the abler, richer men who usually had more than one wife
—remained solidly pagan. They often sucked Christians back into
their pagan polygamous society.

Today Christianity no longer arrives with the political power and
prestige of the imperial European powers. Today more than 5,000
Independent African Churches (denominations) are studying the
Bible themselves and coming to their own decision as to whether
polygamists may be baptized or not. Today the issue as to whether
believers who have more than one wife may be baptized or not is
keener than it ever has been before. The issue is not limited to Africa
by any means. It applies to all societies where plural marriage is
regarded as legitimate. No question is more discussed in missionary
circles than this: what should Churches and missions do in regard to
polygamists who want to become Christians?[8]

—Donald McGavran
Church Growth Bulletin

How crucial is the problem of polygamy to churches and missions? Consider the following facts. Christward movements are gaining strength among the populations of Latin America, Asia, and Africa. Africa south of the Sahara alone is estimated to have more than two hundred million Christians by the year 2000. Dr. David Barrett, after careful study, projects that there will be 357 million Christians by then. Many of those who are in the process of turning to Christian faith come from polygamous cultures. The question of whether or not earnest seekers who have more than one wife should be baptized must be answered, because the growth of the church depends on the turning to Christ of those receptive millions. Is monogamous marriage one of the traditions of the church or one of the revelations of Scripture? What does the Word of God say about the baptism of a man with more than one wife?

The Bible on Polygamy

In the Old Testament, the Word clearly related cases where polygamists were pleasing to God. In the New Testament there is not a chapter, nor a verse, not a word which condemns polygamy or prohibits the baptism of a believing polygamist.

All one can find in the New Testament about polygamy is an inference. Three well known passages—1 Timothy 3:2 and 3:12 and Titus 1:16—list among the qualifications of deacons and elders the stricture that each should be "a husband of one wife." The inference is that in the New Testament Church were men who had two or more wives. These were, moreover, men of sufficiently good standing that, but for Paul's counsel, they might have been chosen for deacons or elders.

Furthermore, "husband of one wife" is stated on a par with other qualifications which these leaders ideally ought to have. Officers of the Church ought to be "temperate," "sensible," "apt teachers," and ought to have children who are "submissive" and are "believers." The Church no doubt has sought such men to be her leaders, but not one of these other qualifications is now or ever has been considered an absolute requirement. Many deacons and elders have been appointed—and I believe correctly appointed, for we have to do the best we can in given circumstances—who are not "apt teachers." Many had children who were not believers or had lapsed. In the Church of Rome, many were appointed who had no children at all and were not husbands of one wife.

Are these passages laying down absolute requirements, or rather did Paul intend them to be counsel concerning virtues desirable in deacons and elders? Do not the verses suggest that as far as possible the Church should choose deacons and elders who possess these qualifications, in at least some measure? It sounds very much as if the Scriptures were saying that married men as a rule make better deacons and elders than unmarried, and that those married to one wife make better church leaders than those married to two or more. (It is possible, of course, to construe the clause which refers to "one woman" more strictly, i.e., to hold that it absolutely prohibits men with more than one wife—or remarried widowers!!—being deacons or elders; but this construction faces the difficulty that the other clauses— apt teachers, submissive children, and the like—are seldom if ever construed absolutely. Why should this one be?)

These three passages then support the position that believing polygamists out of non-Christian society may be baptized. (a) They strongly infer that in the Early Church there were husbands of two or more wives. (b) They may even indicate that in the choice of deacons and elders there was no absolute prohibition of men with two or more wives.

Church rulings on monogamy rest back not on Scripture but on considerations such as these: according to the Scriptures, women are of as great worth as men; polygamy inevitably weighs the balances in favor of the men; since polygamy sequesters large numbers of women with a small number of men and thus leaves multitudes of young men without wives, it encourages adultery among the young men and sex hungry wives of the old men; since numbers of men and women are very nearly equal, the best rule in the matter of marriage is "one man: one woman"; and polygamous households are often torn by jealousies, infidelities, and quarrels. The Church has been right—polygamy is not as good a system as monogamy. Nevertheless, monogamous marriage is one of the traditions of the Church, not one of the revelations of Scripture. It is a *good* tradition which the Church is likely to uphold; but it is a *tradition*. Since Scripture is silent on the issue, the Church which made the tradition is free, within the limits of other germane biblical principles, to adapt it so that it fits temporary conditions in societies becoming Christian for the first time.

This is what many Christians and an increasing number of Churches (denominations) are saying. Among thinking Christians, conviction grows that the Church must say that while this "tradition of the elders" (monogamous marriage) is good for discipled populations, in populations being discipled the tradition (inferred in First Timothy and Titus) which allows believing polygamists to be baptized must be revived. Full membership in the Church of Jesus Christ must not be denied to those who, while yet unbelievers and integral parts of a pre-Christian social order, have legally married more than one wife.[9]

—Donald McGavran
Church Growth Bulletin

Consult Bible commentaries for the elucidation of 1 Timothy 3:2; 3:12; and Titus 1:6. How do you interpret the phrase, "husband of one wife"? Do you agree with the inference that the New Testament church had within its membership some men who were married to more than one woman?

As a matter of fact, the Scriptures remain silent on the issue of polygamy. It seems that we are left with very little to go on. Nevertheless, we must decide what to do about the baptism of millions of receptive polygamists. Anthropology will aid the process of making such a decision. Through insights from anthropology we will know more about the nature of the polygamous system and its relations to other social institutions. Anthropology can tell us how polygamy works within a society.

Anthropological Insights on Polygamy

Missionary anthropologist Alan Tippett explains the cohesiveness of the polygamous system and the inter-relatedness of various social institutions. Each society is self-contained and its social mechanisms are devised to provide for the needs of the society. Before the advent of welfare and retirement programs, the extended family served as a basic unit to meet the needs of its members. In a polygamous society which is highly cohesive, disruption of the familial structure caused by Christianity leaves the abandoned wives and their children destitute. Often prostitution is the only means for their survival. The conversion of polygamists without a provision to care for the accompanying social problems creates confusion and brings about disastrous results. Let us see what Tippett has to say concerning this problem.

In a society without adequate mechanisms for divorce it is quite difficult to change over from polygamy to monogamy. On the other hand, if a way of divorce does exist and the Church resorts to this means of solving the problem of polygamy, she has to justify her support of divorce as a legitimate social institution. This cannot be done on a basis of scriptural exegesis and therefore she has to argue or rationalize her position. Here we get involved in many problems. Is divorce Christian? Is a marriage contract honestly entered into between two parties (regardless of what their religion was at the time) a matter in which they are honor-bound? Is a man, for the sake of Christian baptism, justified in putting away his wives, with whom he has entered into such a contract in good faith, when they desire to continue in the agreed state of wedlock? If the Bible does not supply us with adequate guidance in these matters, on what kind of criteria can the case be reasoned? In point of fact we discover the polygamous system extremely cohesive and this cohesiveness is part of the strength of the society itself. If we are to be social iconoclasts we had better know well just what we are doing.

The polygamous family is not an institutional isolate. Take, for example, a society which practices levirate marriage, and there are scores of them among the currently responsive animistic societies of the mission field. Thus, through the death of his brother, a man (who already has a wife and family) may suddenly find himself with an additional one. Even though he may have become a Christian as the husband of one wife, he is now confronted with the problem of accepting his family responsibilities, which were the basic assumptions of both the individuals and the families involved when the pre-Christian marriage was first contracted. When the new Christian structure forbids the levirate marriage, there emerges in that Christian society a new set of social problems not known previously—the ramifying problems of the widow and the orphan. Christianity has destroyed the social mechanisms which previously provided for the welfare of these persons, and unless some special functional substitute is introduced, these unfortunate people are just not provided for at all. One does not have to travel far through the mission fields of the world to realize the tragic truth of this. What I am really saying, then, is that polygamous human societies normally have a network of interrelated institutions functionally responsible for preserving the perpetuity of the extended family, and the personal security of each individual in them.[10]

—Donald McGavran
Church Growth Bulletin

* * * * *

In view of anthropological insights and Biblical silence concerning polygamy, does it not appear that the strategy the church should employ to abolish polygamy is to prevent further polygamous marriages from happening by first allowing polygamists to become Christians and the polygamous system to run its course and then educating the second generation Christians to adopt a monogamous marriage pattern? What do you think? In the meantime should the church baptize all those receptive millions who are polygamists?

14: PSYCHOLOGY, RECEPTIVITY, AND CHURCH GROWTH

Insights from psychology greatly aid the strategy of church growth. Unfortunately, psychology is the least developed of behavioral sciences for the aid of church growth. Christian psychologists can contribute to the field of church growth by investigating the areas of receptivity, ethnopsychology, decision-making, problem-solving, and internal qualitative Christian growth. Committed Christian individuals are needed to discover the ways in which multitudes of non-Christians can find the Lord of their lives.

Roy Shearer, more than anyone else, has delved into the areas of church growth which psychology is capable of furthering. In the following statement, Shearer explores the idea of receptivity and specifies the need to develop a method of testing situations for recognizing potential responsiveness. Church growth will be greatly furthered when such mechanisms are successfully devised.

Research in church growth has shown that when people are ready to receive the Gospel, they will respond to the most stumbling of presentations. However, people who are not ready to receive the Gospel will reject it even though it is presented with the most brilliant argument and the most sophisticated means available. An extreme example is the high resistance of Moslems in the Middle East to evangelism connected with education, hospitals, or the Gospel presented through literature, radio or any other means. On the other hand, when the inhabitants of certain parts of Indonesia turned receptive, the Gospel ran faster than the professional advocates, because the people passed the Good News on ahead of both the national and foreign missionaries. . . .

Receptivity to new ideas has been studied by the anthropologist Homer G. Barnett . . . Included in his research on all aspects of innovation in his study of the process and causes for acceptance and rejection of new ideas or of innovation. His general description of acceptance is a good account of the process of acceptance of the Gospel. Barnett shows that acceptors to a new idea are basically unsatisfied with their lives as they are; acceptors desire something new. So it is with acceptance of the Gospel. A gospel acceptor has to be unsatisfied with his current life-style before he will change his religious orientation. Barnett . . . finds that there are three characteristics of people ready to receive a new idea: (1) they will receive the new idea only if it satisfies a want better than some existing means; (2) the reception of this idea depends in part on the previous life experience of the person; and (3) dissatisfaction may be a pervasive attitude in some individuals.

H. G. Barnett, *Innovation: Basis of Cultural Change*. New York: McGraw-Hill Book Company, 1953.

Evidence that this theory holds true for the Christian Church is seen in the fact that most of the converts to Christianity in the last century (who were not raised in Christian homes) have not come out of one of the great religions where there was a strong satisfying set of beliefs. Rather, most of the Christians of the new world have been won out of animism, which is not satisfying to the people. Often modern science (including education and medicine) has helped animists to become dissatisfied with their belief in spirits and makes them ready to turn to another religion.

The gospel advocate can promote this dissatisfaction among a population where he wants to effect a religious change. If he can convince his hearers that he has something desirable, then he has produced the want that will lead to receptivity and change.

Often, however, what the advocate says has little bearing on the reason of receptivity. Many people in India became Christians for social reasons; they wanted to better themselves. Pickett . . . shows that they became sound Christians after enumerating a great many different motives for their initial interest in Christianity. Many Koreans turned to Christ because the Church represented a political force to combat the Japanese colonialists. Many people have turned to Christ because of a need for physical healing. The list of reasons is endless. Thus, while the gospel advocate can influence the hearer's dissatisfaction with his own lot, there is overwhelming evidence that men and women have turned to Christ in responding to the preaching about salvation. Those who came were in no way rejected. The important thing is they came and God has used this kind of receptivity to build some strong churches.

If receptivity truly is an important factor in the spread of Christianity, then adequate tests of this receptivity must be produced. Up to the present time the only such adequate test is a growing religious body. Wherever we see a growing church, we can be sure that the people in that area are receptive to religious ideas.

Wherever we see a growing non-Christian religion, we can be sure the people in that place are potential receptors of the Gospel. This test of religious receptivity is useful, but limited because it is a measure after the fact. Many years go by before we can determine if a people are receptive by watching the Church grow.

Is there no better way to test receptivity? Yes, I believe there is a better way but it will take much dedicated, skillful research and much money. Psychologists have long been assessing the attitudes of people. This skill in assessing attitudes should be harnessed for the mission of the Church. A conversion-readiness questionnaire could be carefully constructed with standardization and validation procedures currently used for the best of the nearly two thousand psychological tests available.

> J. Waskom Pickett, *Christian Mass Movements in India.* Lucknow, India: Lucknow Publishing House, 1933.

To be useful, the questionnaire should be scored to read out and estimate (a) the amount of dissatisfaction a person has with his culture, (b) the amount of dissatisfaction he has with his present religion, (c) the strength of bond with his family and clan, (d) the amount of freedom the respondent has to change, and (e) the part his family or clan group plays in a decision to change. Other scales could be discovered during the process of validation which would indicate aspects of receptivity.

If this test were translated into many languages and properly administered with sampling procedures, valuable data for pinpointing the segments of a population that are receptive to change would emerge. The test would also indicate the better approaches for eliciting greatest response. Within segments of a population this test could show which cross-section by age, occupation, or other group is most receptive; church planting could then be aimed at that specific group.[11]

—Roy E. Shearer
from *God, Man and Church Growth*

15: SOCIOLOGY IN CHURCH GROWTH STUDIES

The application of sociological insights to the affairs of the church has been generally neglected. The advocates of church growth, however, strongly believe and have demonstrated that knowledge of sociology greatly aids church growth. The discipline of sociology enlightens human beings in their group relationships. Whatever else it may be, the church is a sociological entity. It is made up of individual human beings taking part in the society at large. Therefore, just as the church can influence the society, the attitudes of the society toward the church can buttress or hinder its activities. Church growth is very much dependent upon an understanding of sociological factors within the societies in which the missionaries work. Some societal elements contribute to church growth while others hinder it. Sociology thus becomes an indispensable tool for those engaged in missionary work.

The present unit discusses the tendency, on the part of Western churches and missions, to ignore the relevancy of sociology for mission and underscores the importance of sociology in church growth studies.

> Western Churches and missions (and national leaders trained by them) commonly ignore sociology. They speak and act as if, for example, all residents of Mexico were equally immersed in a Spanish-speaking middle-class culture. They plan a course of action as if all residents of India were emancipated members of the higher castes. By ignoring social stratification and disregarding homogeneous units and webs of relationship, they constantly diminish the effectiveness of their presentation of Christ.
>
> They do this with the best of intentions. Some of them believe that Christianity (being a religion of brotherhood) cannot afford to recognize separate clans or tribes. In Christ, they exclaim, there is neither Jew nor Greek! Some feel it a great mistake to permit Christianity to be identified with the lower classes, animist tribesmen, the masses, or the illiterate. They therefore engage in only one kind of presentation—to their own peers! Some believe it sufficient to proclaim Christ to men in general. As this is done, they feel, the Great Shepherd will recognize and call His own. "We are resolved to know nothing of homogeneous units and tribes and castes," exclaimed one pastor. "We preach Christ. Those destined for salvation are converted."
>
> Christian mission today is particularly prone to ignore sociological differences because of the confluence of the ecumenical and Africasian [African, Latin American, Asian] emphases. Ecumenicists are vigorously engaged in building bridges of understanding between denominations and look with horror on any further division of the

Body of Christ into separate Churches. Afericasian Christians have little sympathy with Eurican [European, North American] denominational peculiarities (be these Angelican, Roman Catholic, or Baptist). Facing non-Christian religions, Afericasians tend to think of themselves as simply Christian and to love the strength which comes with unity.

Whatever the reasons, a clear-cut recognition of the fragmented character of society, a realistic acceptance of the fact that some populations are more responsive than others, and a skilled proclamation of the Gospel to the peoples whom God has prepared, is often lacking. In investigations of church growth in many lands, we have found that recognition of the sociological matrix is a key factor. The lack of this recognition is one of the most crucial issues in church growth today.

Recognizing the principle that "each piece of the mosaic develops a Church which grows best at its own rate and flourishes under its own leaders" does not necessarily clash with either the ecumenical or Afericasian emphasis. Just as the Methodist Church in Brazil is a different administrative unit from the Methodist Church in Chile, and these both in turn from the Methodist Church in Angola, so the linguistic and ethnic differences can be recognized and used as

> ## SOCIETY AS A MOSAIC
>
> The general population may be compared to a mosaic. Each piece of the mosaic is a society, a homogeneous unit. It has its own way of life, its own standards, degree of education, self-image, and places of residence. Even city "melting pots" on examination turn out to be a series of wards or neighborhoods, each occupied by a different homogeneous unit.[12]
>
> —Donald McGavran
> *Church Growth and Christian Mission*

highways of the Spirit without breaking the unity of the Church. In 1910 the Anglican Church in India was one Church, but it had a separate diocese for Chhota Nagpur, precisely so that the Uraon and Munda Church there might grow up under its own leaders, facing its own problems and adjusting itself to the unique opportunity to multiply churches among the Uraons and Mundas. With the increasing Christianization of peoples and the continual erosion of local peculiarities, the need for separate administrative machinery (separate Churches) will diminish, not increase. We need neither fear nor fight it.[13]

—Donald McGavran
Church Growth and Christian Mission

16: SOCIAL STRUCTURES, DECISION-MAKING, AND CHURCH GROWTH

A sociological scheme which expresses the structural change from a basically agrarian orientation to an industrial-urban one is the well known *Gemeinschaft-Gesellschaft* contrast. The following lists characterize the "community" and "association" attributes.

Gemeinschaft (community)	*Gesellschaft* (association)
primary group relations	secondary group relations
face-to-face, total relationships with each other (as in the family and village)	a set of relations with the participants presenting only one specialized part of their social personalities (roles) to each other
more rural	more urban
pre-industrial	industrial
the individual swallowed up in group life where the communal principle dominates social relationships	the individual free to choose
emphasis on collectivity-orientations	emphasis on self-orientations
non-Western societies	Western societies

The structural change from the communal to the associational type of society involves a fundamental shift in the relationship of the individual to his group. In a traditional agrarian society, he does not make decisions without first consulting the group norms. He is not free to make his own decisions. The interests and aspirations of his primary social group override those of his own. In a more industrialized society, the individual is free from the restrictions of the communal life to make his own decisions.

Social Structures and Decision-Making

The social structure of a people is an important factor in determining how innovations, such as new religions, are accepted. In western society each person is encouraged to make decisions on his own without consulting others. This cultural trait is strengthened

81

through the breakdown of the wider family into independent nuclear units and through great mobility. The evangelism which works best in this kind of social structure is one which seeks individual conversions.

But western social structure with its fragmented society is unique among the societies of the world. The social structure of most peoples . . . has solidarity and interdependence. Decisions are not usually made without consulting others. Evangelism in societies of this kind, to be effective, must aim at winning social units by encouraging internal discussion and informal vote-taking until these units are won for Christ.[14]

—Gilbert W. Olson
Church Growth in Sierra Leone

Social Structure and Church Growth

The rate of growth is . . . often closely dependent upon the structure of the society in question. If, for example, a Church is witnessing to a face-to-face society (one in which most of the people of a village, town, or tribelet know one another), it usually either reaches the entire group or splits the society along clan or family lines . . . In Latin America, for example, a number of churches in small towns and villages tend to grow rapidly to the size of 50 to 100 members, but almost immediately thereafter growth stops, and for a number of years there may be little or no increase. A careful study of such churches reveals that in many instances the church has

THE BIBLICAL AWARENESS OF SOCIAL STRUCTURE

The incarnation of the Son of God (Philippians 2:7, 8) was within the social limitations of Judaism, even within a specific lineage within that nation. With respect to locale, it emerged within a normal Galilean village structure, within an occupational group in the peasant economy, where Jesus lived as a carpenter and the son of a carpenter (Matthew 13:55; Mark 6:3). His speech also, it would seem, followed the linguistic enclosure of his own people: he probably spoke in the Galilean Aramaic dialect, which was so distinct that it caused comment by the townspeople as near as Jerusalem (Mark 14:70). Jesus himself was known as a countryman and was spoken of as the "prophet of Nazareth" (Matthew 21:10, 11). Yet he was sent as the Father's herald to proclaim salvation to all—"whosoever believeth" (John 3:16). Within the social enclosure of Jewish life, language, and custom, Jesus dealt not only with individuals but with kin groups, both he and the Gospel writers recognizing their entity: the Zebedee family (Mark 1:19); Lazarus and his sisters (John 11 and 12); classes of people like the 'publicans and sinners' (Luke 15:2; Mark 2:16); village groups, such as those at Cana (John 2:1) and Capernaum (v. 12), drawn together for a festival; occupational groups, like the Bethsaida fishermen (1:44); racial groups (4:40); and huge mixed crowds. He sent his disciples to households and villages (Luke 8:1; 10:5, 8, 9, etc.).

The apostles were also alert to *winnable* social segments—they planted household churches (Philemon 2, etc.), itinerated

grown to include almost all the members of one dominant family, including the various ramifications by birth, marriage, and godfather relationships. But when a church is built around one family, it is rare that any equally important family will come in. In fact, in many situations the most critical time in the growth of such a church is the point at which it has included most of the members of one family, but has not succeeded in attracting influential members of other important families. Family connections can thus be not only bridges for growth but also blind alleys of stagnation. . . .

In an urban society, church growth is more likely to follow geographical, occupational, and friendship lines than family ones. Thus, in a class-divided urban society, Protestant churches are likely to consist primarily of a single class. This is so not only because birds of a feather flock together, but also because interpersonal communication, which in social structures is primarily within a class rather than between classes, is much more likely to be effective within a single class structure.[15]

—Eugene A. Nida
Church Growth and Christian Mission

through villages (Acts 9:35) and towns (9:42; 10:24, etc.), traveled from district to district and land to land (as, for example, the journeys of Paul). They paid attention to craft groups (18:3), penetrated some intellectual segments (17:32-34), won even magicians in great numbers (19:19) and groups in political employment (Philippians 4:22, in Caesar's household).[16]

—A. R. Tippett
Church Growth and the Word of God

* * * * *

1. Discuss what might transpire in the experience of an individual involved in the process of transition from one type of society to another. The concept of modernization is used to describe this structural change in society. What in your opinion are the ill effects of moderniza-

tion and what advantages and disadvantages do they present to the church in its evangelistic effort?

2. What is the pattern of decision-making in America? You ordinarily consult your parents, close friends, and others whom you respect, but in the final analysis you are on your own to make the decision with or without counsel from others. This is not the case in most non-Western countries. One's becoming a Christian often means riding against the tide and involves considerable sacrifices and dangers. Can you imagine yourself becoming a Buddhist, a Communist, or a Hindu? And yet is this not exactly the same as one's becoming a Christian in a non-Western, non-Christian, highly communal society?

3. Comment on the following statement: "In an urban society, church growth is more likely to follow geographical, occupational, and friendship lines than family ones." Does your observation of American church memberships confirm the statement?

17: HOMOGENEOUS UNITS AND CHURCH GROWTH

Each society is made up of numerous social units with characteristics of their own. The persons comprising a social unit have much in common and what they share in common distinguishes them from other social units in the society. For this reason, McGavran uses the phrase *a homogeneous unit* referring to that cohesive segment within the society.

THE LANGUAGE OF THE HEART

Hundreds of millions of men live in two worlds. The first, of great importance to them, is that of "our intimates who speak our own language"; the second, of relatively slight importance, is that world of a strange tongue in which we trade and work with outsiders. In the first the "medium of communication" is the language of the heart; in the second, the "medium of confusion" is a trade language or standard language, good enough for buying and selling, taking orders and finding one's way, but pitifully inadequate for the things that really matter. Men fight, make love, and mourn in their mother tongue.

Because the only way modern nation-states can function is to create a citizenry all of whose members speak one language, governments and education departments work ceaselessly to propagate standard languages and to eliminate what they call dialects (some of which are languages in their own right). The standard language is the key to unity. Nevertheless, the language of the heart is difficult to stamp out. It is learned from the mother's lips and spoken in the home. It is an inner sanctuary where the outside world cannot penetrate. It is jealously guarded because it enhances a sense of peoplehood. . . .

As the Church spreads throughout the earth, she is constantly dealing with hundreds of millions who live in these two worlds. In some cases she speaks the heart language and flourishes, in others she pre-

HOMOGENEOUS UNIT DEFINED

The *homogeneous unit* is simply a section of society in which all the members have some characteristic in common.[17]

—Donald McGavran
Understanding Church Growth

sents the Gospel in a standard language and languishes. Where it appears that the 'dialect' is going to die out and the standard language is the one in which Bible and hymnbook are available, government carries on its business, and schools do their work, there it seems reasonable for the Church to preach, pray, sing, and read the Bible, not in the potent language of the heart but in the important language of the future. It may be reasonable and cheap, but it is seldom effective. However, it must be said that such is the power of the Gospel and so many are the other factors that impel men to become disciples of Christ, that frequently the Church grows despite this handicap. That it is a handicap should never be forgotten.[18]

—Donald McGavran
Understanding Church Growth

Language, for example, is one of the most important distinguishing traits, and even the casual observer recognizes that the sixteen tribes in Liberia have sixteen different languages and are therefore sixteen homogeneous units. . . .

That the tribe is a homogeneous unit is obvious. Multiple sub-groupings are not so obvious, but are often more significant for church growth. These smaller groupings are even more homogeneous than the tribe—that is, the members have closer ties and more attributes in common. Some of these unifying traits may be based on location, e.g., a village, or a "quarter" in a village. Some of the divisions are based on kinship, such as extended family or clan. In some cases economic circumstances such as poverty or dependence on a particular occupation are the unifying factors. More often several of these elements in combination unite the group.

Each homogeneous unit has a strong people consciousness. When a man considers becoming a Christian he always thinks of the effect it will have on his tribal relationships, his kinsmen, and his way of life. Some groupings are effectively hidden from the missionary because there is nothing corresponding to them in his own culture. The ties of clan or extended family are likely to seem unnecessarily complex or foolishly arbitrary to the uninitiated Westerner. But for evangelism they may be the most significant of all.[20]

—Joseph Conrad Wold
*God's Impatience
in Liberia*

For Further Study—
J. Waskom Pickett, *Christian Mass Movements in India.* Lucknow, India: Lucknow Publishing House, 1933.

CHURCH GROWTH AND THE GEOGRAPHICAL LOCATION

Throughout Hindu India, the depressed-class ward has been separated from the rest of the village by physical distance—often a hundred yards or more. As people of these wards became Christian and pastors were appointed to shepherd them, the separate location posed a problem to missions. Should the pastor—an educated, respectable Christian—live in the Untouchable ward or seek quarters in the upper-caste section of the village? Arguing that it would help Christians more if their pastor lived in a respectable part of the town, missions in North India located their pastors there. Arguing that the pastor's place was with his people, missions in South India located him in the Untouchable ward itself. Pickett observes that the South India procedure (its use of the social structure) was much more successful in terms of creating a genuine Christian Church.[19]

—Donald McGavran
Understanding Church Growth

PEOPLE CONSCIOUSNESS AND CHURCH GROWTH

A homogeneous unit of society may be said to have 'people consciousness' when its members think of themselves as a separate tribe, caste, or class. Thus the Orthodox Jews in Eurica have high people consciousness, as do the castes in India, the Indian tribes in Ecuador, and many other societies in many lands.

Give an example of a homogeneous unit within your own community and explain the homogeneity of that social unit by delineating the culture traits which its members share in common.

The gospel is said to spread most rapidly within the homogeneous units. Why do you think this is so?

The homogeneous units think and act as a group. What implications do you find the concept of the homogeneous unit to have on the people movement and group conversion?

The degree of people consciousness is an aspect of social structure which greatly influences when, how, and to what extent the Gospel will flow through that segment of the social order. Castes or tribes with high people consciousness will resist the Gospel primarily because to them becoming a Christian means "joining another people." They refuse Christ not for religious reasons, not because they love their sins, but precisely because they love their brethren. . . .

It may be taken as axiomatic that whenever becoming a Christian is considered a racial rather than a religious decision, there the growth of the Church will be exceedingly slow. As the Church faces the evangelization of the world, perhaps her main problem is how to present Christ so that men can truly follow Him without traitorously leaving their kindred.

The only solutions to this problem to date are: (a) to wait till the society disintegrates, people consciousness grows low, a melting pot develops, or the military might of a conqueror destroys pride of peoplehood; and (b) to enable men and women to become Christians in groups while still remaining members of their tribe, caste, or people. Where Christians can continue marrying among their own kind, attending each other's weddings and funerals, and maintaining close connection with their non-Christian brethren, there the Church can grow both fast and soundly.[21]

—Donald McGavran
Understanding Church Growth

Chapter 4
APPLYING SCIENTIFIC CONCEPTS
TO CHURCH GROWTH

That insights from behavioral sciences aid church growth in understanding its dynamics has been shown in the previous chapter. Anthropology, especially cultural anthropology, enables the missionary to see the people whom he serves and their patterns of behavior in a unique cultural setting, thereby furthering church growth by avoiding common pitfalls often committed in cross-cultural activity. Though much remains to be explored, psychology can advance church growth by specifying receptivity. Sociology enlightens men and women in their group relationships. Men in tightly homogeneous societies respond to the gospel differently from those in more individualistic societies. For the sake of expanding God's kingdom on earth, the church cannot afford to ignore the insights from behavioral sciences. The church can and should appropriate such insights to greater growth.

The present chapter applies scientific concepts to describing church growth. It will explain the scientific process of research in defining a project, delineating the facts to be gathered for the measurement of church growth, and analyzing the causes which, in fact, have produced or hindered the growth. Since one learns best how to do research by doing it, the chapter contains a diagnostic exercise.

18: UNDERSTANDING THE SCIENTIFIC PROCESS OF RESEARCH

The purpose of research is to apply scientific concepts and procedures in order to answer carefully defined questions. The questions, however, must be of such nature that observation or experimentation in the natural world can provide the needed information. In an attempt to pinpoint the growth which God has blessed, church growth researchers deal with scientifically observable data. McGavran gives his rationale for the use of the numerical approach in analyzing these data.

> The numerical approach is essential to understanding church growth. The Church is made up of countable people and there is nothing particularly spiritual in not counting them. Men use the numerical approach in all worthwhile human endeavor. Industry, commerce, finance, research, government, invention and a thousand other lines of enterprise derive great profit and much of their stability in development from continual measurement. Without it they would feel helpless and blindfolded. The vast programs of education, to which advances in every country owe so much, employ numerical procedures at every turn. The counting of pupils by sex and grade, place of residence and intellectual ability, and degree of learning and rates of progress is never questioned. Without it, effective administration and accurate forecasts would be impossible.
>
> It is common to scorn church statistics—but this is part of the fog. This cheap scorn, casting about for biblical support, sometimes finds that God was displeased with King David for taking a census of the people (2 Samuel 24:1-10), conveniently overlooking many chapters of Numbers in which God commands a meticulous numbering of all Israel and every part of every tribe. "Take ye the sum of all the congregation of the children of Israel, after their families, by the house of their fathers, with the number of their names, every male by their polls; from twenty years old and upward, all that are able to go forth to war in Israel: thou and Aaron shall number them by their armies" (Numbers 1:2, 3). Also overlooked is Luke's great emphasis on numbers in the book of Acts and his careful record of the numerical increase of the Church . . . On biblical grounds one has to affirm that devout use of the numerical approach is in accord with God's wishes. On practical grounds, it is as necessary in congregations and denominations as honest financial dealing.
>
> To be sure, no one was ever saved by statistics; but then, no one was ever cured by the thermometer to which a physician pays such close attention. X-ray pictures never knit a single broken bone, yet they are of considerable value to physicians in telling them how to put the two ends of a fractured bone together. Similarly, the facts of

growth will not in themselves lead anyone to Christ. But they can be of marked value to any Church which desires to know where, when, and how to carry on its work so that maximum increase of soundly Christian churches will result.[1]

—Donald McGavran
Understanding Church Growth

Research is generally conducted for two reasons. One is for the sake of knowing or understanding. This satisfies the *intellectual* desire to know or understand something. The other is more *practical.* One wishes to know or understand for the sake of being able to do something more efficiently. The former is called pure or basic research and the latter applied research. In church growth no research should be conducted (at the expense of the church's money) only for the sake of knowing. Church growth studies are carried on in order to discover what growth God has granted and the factors which He has used to obtain that growth "so that maximum increase of soundly Christian churches will result."

During the years church growth researchers have undertaken various pieces of study which are now categorized and described as "models for missiological research." (See Chapter 2, Unit 11.) Models call for specific methods of research. In the main, church growth research to date has heavily depended on case studies. McGavran, in his Jamaican study, has this to say:

> The church grows differently in each population and needs accurate assessment. Church growth is a many-sided process. No formula for it exists. The task therefore is to describe the precise Church which God has built in each specific population, and the ploughing, sowing, weeding, and reaping, which have brought these particular sheaves into the Master's storehouse. Since each Church has its own individuality, founding mission and *heilgeschichte,* this means hundreds of careful descriptions. These writings on church growth should be done by many . . . they should all bind themselves to a single task—describing the physical increase of the Church.[2]

One may study the growth of a given denomination in a given country during a period of time, as did Roy E. Shearer on the Presbyterians in Korea or Lloyd E. Kwast on the Baptists in West Cameroon. Generally, however, case studies in church growth utilize the comparative method as a tool of research. McGavran speaks of the desirability of this method.

> In these days, study of growth of other Churches than our own is not merely possible but highly desirable. No one can afford to neglect the comparative study of church growth. It uncovers a rich vein of knowledge concerning how churches grow, and increases under-

standing of God's purposes for His Church and the methods He is blessing to their increase.[3]

Thus church growth researchers apply the comparative method to church growth studies. McGavran continues to describe the methodology.

> The basic methodology for study of other Churches is the same as that used in studying one's own. Secure accurate figures for communicant membership and other pertinent data across the years. Refine the data to eliminate statistical errors and redefinitions. Make sure all the figures are for the same geographical unit. Draw accurate graphs portraying growth histories. Dig out from histories, biographies, interviews, and reports the reasons for growth or decline shown in each graph of each denomination. Check all thinking about church growth against the graphs.[4]

The emphasis on case studies is well placed, since sound church growth theory can be built only on solid case studies conducted among specific populations in numerous countries. The procedure for church growth research must now be stated.

Any descriptive study of church growth should contain the following three steps:

1. Defining the study—a carefully defined statement of the purpose and scope of your research project. For example, Yamamori, defining his study of the churches in Japan, writes: "The purpose of the study was to describe and analyze the growth and development of eight Protestant denominations founded in Japan before 1900 by identifying the factors which made for the growth, or non-growth, for the period between 1859 and 1939."[5] The statement makes clear the purpose and scope of his study. The purpose of the study was "to describe and analyze the growth and development" of the churches "by identifying the factors which made for the growth, or non-growth." The churches being studied were also specified. Not only were there "eight" Protestant denominations for the sake of comparison but more specifically, they were those denominations founded in Japan before 1900. The churches to be compared must have existed during the same period within the same population. The eight churches were among the same population because the Japanese are homogeneous. Much of the success in research depends on the way the problem is formulated and the study defined.

2. After defining the study, the next step would be measuring church growth. Without a clear picture of what growth has taken place, one cannot analyze the causes for that growth. Membership

facts of the churches being studied must be obtained and their accuracy scrutinized against the most reliable sources available. Then, membership facts must be plotted on a graph. This graph will be an outline of the growth history of the churches.

3. The final step will be testing the causes against the graph. The graph will show the periods of rapid and slow growth. The researcher's assignment is to discover the causes which contributed to the rapid growth of certain churches while others declined in the same period. What factors make for growth? Some diagnostic tools and sources are available and will be discussed. The following units will take up Steps 2 and 3.

* * * * *

1. What is your response to McGavran's rationale for the use of the numerical approach?

2. List some of the "scientific observable data" related to the church—its membership and activities.

3. Think of three problems in American church growth. Define them.

19: MEASURING CHURCH GROWTH

In the study of church growth, confusion sometimes occurs as to what is being measured. Whatever is to be measured must be in fact measurable. To avoid unnecessary confusion, Yamamori defines the terms "church" and "growth" in the following statement.

> While the church, as a divine society, draws its inner courage from the grace of God revealed in Christ and constantly made available by the Holy Spirit, it nevertheless exists in time and space and is composed of men and women vulnerable to human influences and environment. In other words, the church, among other things, is a sociological entity subject to analysis by the principles used in the study of all human institutions. Only by defining the church as being made up of concrete individuals taking part in the society at large, the study of church growth becomes possible.
>
> The term "growth" indicates an increase of membership constituency composed of men and women who can be counted. Admittedly, this is not the only way in which the church is commonly known to grow. For one example, the church like any special group grows in its creedal and organizational aspects which are pursued primarily by the theologians and historians of the church. While these aspects received our attention insofar as they influenced the physical expansion of the church, they did not serve our purpose of becoming the objective criterion by which the growth of the church was measured. They inevitably involve theological and ecclesiastical value judgments which would cause never-ending arguments centering on the nature of the church and the norms of the Christian faith. For another, the church—its membership—is said to grow qualitatively in patience, humility, kindness, obedience, faithfulness, hope and love. These are the qualities which are measured only by God and not by men. These no doubt influence the kinds of numerical growth obtained, but they themselves cannot be the criteria by which church growth is measured.[6]

The criterion of church growth, then, refers to an increase of church members. Yet, this criterion needs a further explanation. Nida pinpoints the problem:

> Even if we restrict ourselves to so-called statistical growth, we really do not know how to count, for in the opinion of some persons one must count only baptized believers (that is, adults), while other church leaders insist that if one is to obtain an accurate view of the significance of the Christian witness it is not only legitimate but necessary to count the total number of persons in the Christian community.[7]

The question of who among the members should be counted is a difficult one to answer. There are not only nuclear (most active) members but also marginal (least active) ones within any congregation. Should we count only the most active members and not the others? Furthermore, should we count only the baptized adults and not their dependents? What should be the standard of measurement for church membership? The best single measure of the size of a denomination is the category used by missionary statisticians who compiled the *World Atlas of Christian Missions* (1911), *World Missionary Atlas* (1925), and *Interpretative Statistical Survey of the World Mission* (1938). It is called "communicants" meaning "baptized members in good standing" which excludes catechumens, inquirers, sympathizers, church attenders who are not baptized believers, and infants who have been baptized.

Once the criterion of measuring church growth is defined, facts regarding church membership must be gathered. To get a clear picture of what church growth has taken place in a given field, one must obtain (1) *field totals* during the years for the denomination he is studying. The field refers to a geographical boundary delineated in the definition of a research project. The field total may mean the total members of the Episcopal church in the city of Tokyo, in the district of Kanto, or in the nation of Japan. It is beneficial to gather field totals of several denominations in a given field for comparison. (2) Since the church generally grows within a homogeneous unit, *homogeneous unit totals* during the years must be obtained. Homogeneous units must first be identified in a given field and then facts about membership in each homogeneous unit procured. How has the church grown among the Jews in the United States? Among the Mandarin-speaking Chinese in Formosa? Among the Chokosl tribe in Ghana? (3) *Membership figures for individual congregations* during the years reveal the real source of growth for a given denomination and are essential for accurate church growth analyses.

* * * * *

In order to gain a clear picture of how the church is growing in your city, obtain membership figures of your local church for the past ten years. How many sister churches are in the city? How have they grown during the same period? Does your church's growth pattern differ from those of the sister churches? In what way? Can you identify the homogeneous units in the city? Is any one of your sister churches making a notable inroad among any of the homogeneous units? Construct a membership chart of your church for the past ten

years. Do the same for at least five sister churches. Plot
these membership statistics on a graph.

★ ★ ★ ★ ★

FILL IN A MEMBERSHIP CHART:

	−10	−9	−8	−7	−6	−5	−4	−3	−2	Last Year	This Year
Your Church											
Sister Church A											
Sister Church B											
Sister Church C											
Sister Church D											
Sister Church E											

NOTE: Consult the pastor of each congregation for the membership records. Denominational yearbooks contain the membership
statistics by individual churches and by fields or countries. In the
case of compiling homogeneous unit totals, consult mission sec-
retaries, bishops, and mission board headquarters staff. World-wide
mission statistics are readily obtainable by examining the following:

1856 Newcomb, Harvey (Ed.), *A Cyclopedia of Missions—
Containing a Comprehensive View of Missionary Operations Throughout the World.* New York, Scribner.

1891 Bliss, Edward Munsell, *Encyclopaedia of Missions.* Vols. I
and II. New York, London, Funk and Wagnalls.

1901 Beach, Harlan Page, *A Geography and Atlas of Protestant
Missions.* New York, Student Volunteer Movement. Two
volumes.

1911 Dennis, James S., Beach, Harlan P., Fahs, Charles H. (Eds.),
World Atlas of Christian Missions. New York, Student Volunteer Movement for Foreign Missions.

1925 Beach, Harlan P., and Fahs, Charles H. (Eds.), *World Missionary Atlas.* New York, Institute of Social and Religious
Research.

1938 Parker, Joseph I. (Ed.), *Interpretative Statistical Survey of
the World Mission of the Christian Church.* New York, London, International Missionary Council.

1949 Grubb, Kenneth, and Bingle, E. J. (Eds.), *World Christian
Handbook.* London, World Dominion.

1952 Grubb, Kenneth, and Bingle, E. J. (Eds.), *World Christian Handbook.*

1957 Bingle, E. J., and Grubb, Kenneth (Eds.), *World Christian Handbook.*

1962 Coxill, H. Wakelin, and Grubb, Kenneth (Eds.), *World Christian Handbook.*

1968 Coxill, H. Wakelin, and Grubb, Kenneth (Eds.), *World Christian Handbook.*

1970 Missionary Research Library/Missions Advanced Research and Communication Center, *North American Protestant Ministries Overseas Directory.* (9th edition)

1972 MARC, *Mission Handbook: North American Protestant Ministries Overseas* (10th edition).

CONSTRUCT A GRAPH OF YOUR CHURCH IN COMPARISON WITH FIVE SISTER CHURCHES:

MEMBERSHIP

YEARS

20: TESTING THE CAUSES AGAINST THE GRAPH

Compiling membership statistics and plotting them on graphs are not exercises in ecclesiastical pride for the church's accomplishments. They have meaning only insofar as they reveal the outlines of the growth structure such as plateaus, gradual or sudden rises, and sharp declines, so that the factors causing such phenomena might be discovered and utilized for the expansion of the church. Only by constantly testing these causes against the actual graph of growth can one expect to arrive at the reasons why a particular church in a given field has grown.

In the process of discovering the growth factors, several sources are available. There are no easy answers. Superficial explanations must be discarded against the facts of growth.

1. *Examine the written records.* Books and articles written by anthropologists and sociologists provide the background material of the country. The researcher must know the changes that have taken place in the land during the years. Does the traditional *milieu* dominate the behavior patterns of the people? How industrialized is the country? Are the people open to Western influences? Government census reports help describe the status of the country. Mission and church publications contain reports from the field. Reasons for church growth for particular periods are often given. Theses and dissertations deal with the histories of denominational missions and are worth investigating.

2. *Interview those who were there* and know intimately the affairs of the church in the period of study. Question national pastors and missionaries about specific periods of growth and decline. Laymen also can often provide astute observations concerning church growth. Inquire why Church X continued to grow during a certain period while Church Y leveled off.

3. *Conduct diagnostic research.* Several analyses described below reveal the patterns of church growth. The researcher must learn to administer such analyses expeditiously and should be able to summarize and report the findings.

Family Analysis. What does a family analysis reveal? McGavran says:

A family analysis of the congregation reveals the number of *full families* (where husband and wife are both Christians), *half families* (where only one partner is Christian), and *singles*. Obviously a congregation of 34 composed of four full families, seventeen half families, and nine singles is much weaker than a congregation of 34 made up of twelve full families and ten of their believing children. Theoretically, the first congregation has much greater contact with the "outside," but in practice this contact leaves it much more open to erosion. How half families come about is also important and should be ascertained. Sometimes they arise as out of non-Christian families only one partner becomes a believer. In other cases they arise as Christians marry non-Christians. In some cases half families bring loss to the Church and in others the believing partner wins the unbelieving. Much depends on the fervency of the believers and much on other factors.[8]

One of the critical issues facing the church in Japan is membership leakage. With emphasis on the school approach, the church in Japan has gained its membership largely by the conversion of students and single young adults. Since the converts enter the church one by one without the support of familial ties, the drop-out rate is pitifully high. A family analysis in this case pinpoints the vulnerable spot within the structure of the church for which the church must find a solution.

Age Distribution Analysis at the Time of Baptism. In each congregation you visit, go through the membership roster to find the date of birth and the date of adult baptism (or confirmation in the case of the person who previously received an infant baptism). These facts are ordinarily recorded on the roster. From these dates, you can calculate the age at which a member was baptized. Suppose you conduct this simple but tedious research on ten churches in the same region. You will probably have more than one thousand persons with an average of one hundred members in each congregation. Your investigation will reveal the most responsive age bracket. Ask yourself and others why the persons in this particular age bracket respond to the Gospel. What prevents the people in other age brackets from accepting Christ in this particular society?

Analysis of Ways Into and Out of the Church. The following conversation between Donald McGavran and Win Arn dramatizes the basic ways in which people come into and go out of the church.

> McGAVRAN Churches grow in three ways—biological growth, transfer growth and conversion growth. By biological church growth, I mean that which takes place within the family. A man and his wife who are true Christians have, let us say, three children. These grow up, confess Christ, and are added to the church. There are now five Christians. This is biological growth—good and important! The Bible commands us to rear our children in the fear and admonition of the Lord. However, biological growth will never win the world for Christ.

> ARN What growth rate in the church might be expected by biological means?

McGAVRAN This depends upon the rate of growth of the population. In some parts of the world twenty percent a decade, or two percent a year. In America, with its emphasis on family planning and limited population increase, it will be less. Growth rate also depends on the mobility of a community, but in any case, biological growth is not a large growth. A church which depended only on this growth would be committing suicide!

ARN There are too many "dead" churches now. We don't need any suicides. What about transfer growth?

McGAVRAN Transfer growth is that which takes place when people move from one area to another, from the country to the city, or vice versa. The city churches grow larger, and the rural churches grow smaller. That's transfer church growth. If I change a five-dollar bill from one pocket to another, one pocket gets fatter while the other pocket gets leaner, yet my total wealth remains the same.

ARN Transfer growth always means increase for one church and decrease for another, so there has really been no growth in the overall body of Christ.

McGAVRAN Transfer growth is good growth. We should make sure that those who leave one church are brought into the fellowship of another. However, here again, transfer growth will not win the world to Christ.

ARN Transfer growth will make a church look as if it's growing.

McGAVRAN But it's deceptive. The pastor who is simply gathering up incoming Christians and adding them to his church feels good about it, but he has not really added to the church at large.
That brings me to the third kind of church growth, which I call conversion growth, when people come to know Jesus Christ for the first time. Conversion growth is the only kind that really adds significantly to the church.

ARN If we would grow, the focus of effort should be on winning people through conversion.

McGAVRAN Yes, no question about it. Every church should aim for conversion growth. Even though it might have considerable increase by transfer and biological growth, a church should not be satisfied unless it is growing by conversion. Without conversions, the church in the United States will go steadily downhill.

ARN Do you think someone might ask, "But if we go on converting people, won't we soon run out?"

McGAVRAN A Southern Baptist friend of mine used to say expansively, when he was contemplating the spectacular growth his denomination was achieving, "Well, by 1990 there'll be more Southern Baptists in the United States than there are people!" Seriously, tremendous numbers of people are living apart from Christ. They never darken the door of a church. In some communities only ten percent of the population are practicing Christians; in others, possibly fifty percent are. That still leaves huge numbers in the United States who neither know Christ nor love Him.

ARN Let me underscore that—if we want wholesome growth, our focus must be on people who need to know Jesus Christ.

McGAVRAN Exactly!

ARN If there's value in knowing the ways people come into a church, there must also be value in knowing the ways people leave the church.

McGAVRAN Yes. This information is helpful because it tells where the back doors are. People leave the church through death, transfer, and falling away, and we need to know which of these is the major cause. Furthermore, we need to know what ages are losing interest and what groups are falling away. Is it the new members who join the church and within six months are gone? Or is it the youth, or the older members who no longer find the church meeting their needs? We need to know why individuals leave the church, also why groups leave. Once we have this information, we can do something about it. Until then, we have only a vague feeling that everything is not well with the church.[9]

Other Helpful Analyses. The physical outline of a congregation becomes clearer when facts are obtained concerning the age spread, geographical locations, and occupations of the members. The congregation may have a proportionate spread of all age levels. On the other hand, it may be lopsided. In either case, the implications for church growth must be considered. The geographical distribution of members has also church growth implications. How far do the members live from the church? How long does it take for them to come to church? How far or near do they live from each other? The members must live in proximity to the church and to each other in order to keep the Christian fellowship alive and lively. The pastoral and evangelistic efforts of the church may be spread too thin to be effective. An occupational analysis of the congregation likewise sheds light on its growth potential along its homogeneity. A predominantly white-collar congregation will likely gain its future members from the same class. Investigate the occupations of the converts for the past three to five years in a congregation and see if there is any correlation between the church's occupational types and those of the converts.

* * * * *

With each of the congregations you study, divide the additions and losses for the past ten years into their basic categories. Continue to do the same with other congregations in the same region until some patterns emerge.

21: A DIAGNOSTIC EXERCISE

Teaching a student about the methods of church growth research without the actual experience is like teaching a student to swim without water. The purpose of this unit then is for the student to gain competency in church growth research by studying a local congregation. You are to describe and analyze the growth of Church X in an American city. The procedure will be the same in analyzing any congregation throughout the world.

While the current exercise concentrates on a single congregation, the factors affecting its growth or lack of growth will become more evident when other churches in the same area are studied in comparison by the same method.

* * * * *

I. Study the background of Church X.

A. Studies of the area noting major industries, population composition, social structure, city zoning, trends in residential development, educational institutions, and religious climate. Sources: Chamber of Commerce, superintendent of schools, utility research department, sociology departments of area colleges, public library, city planning commission, public health officer, highway department, local newspaper staff.

B. A brief history of Church X, including the circumstances of its founding.

II. Compile membership facts. After filling in the chart, plot the communicant figures for a decade on a graph.

Communicant and Baptismal Figures for the Past Decade

	−10	−9	−8	−7	−6	−5	−4	−3	−2	Last Year	This Year
Communicants											
Baptisms											

III. Conduct diagnostic research and then give reasons for the growth or lack of growth in the congregation.

A. Administer the Membership Analysis Inquiry Sheet. Go over the church roster with the pastor and find information on the following items.

MEMBERSHIP ANALYSIS INQUIRY SHEET

Name of member	Sex	Marital Status	Birth	Baptized in Year	Relation to Others in Church	Profession

KEY: *Sex*
  M - male
  F - female

Marital Status
  S - single
  M - married
  W - widowed
  D - divorced

Birth
  the year each member was born

Baptized in Year—the year each member was baptized as an adult or confirmed (in the case of the person who previously received an infant baptism).

Relation to Others in Church—give relationship of member to others in the congregation.

Profession—give profession of member including housewife and student categories.

Upon the completion of the above inquiry, summarize your findings according to the following categories.

1. Family analysis.

MARITAL STATUS AND SEX DISTRIBUTION

STATUS / CHURCH	FULL FAMILIES		HALF FAMILIES		SINGLES M		SINGLES F		WID—OWED		DI—VORCED		TOTAL		
	Mem-bers	(Cou-ples)	Hus-bands	Wives	Blw 30	Abv 31	Blw 30	Abv 31	M	F	M	F	M	F	Per Church
"X"															
"Y"															
"Z"															

2. Age distribution at the time of baptism. From the dates of birth and adult baptism you can compute the age of each member at which he was baptized. Specify the age brackets responsive to the gospel.

3. Age distribution analysis. Does Church X have a proportionate spread of all age levels? How are the ages represented in the congregation on the basis of the current year?

4. Occupational analysis. What is the occupational composition of Church X? Is the majority of its members engaged in so-called blue-collar work? What trend do you see among the recent converts?

B. Ways into and out of the church analysis. Compare the current membership roster with one dated three or five years ago.

1. Ways into the church. Those persons listed in the current roster, but unlisted in the dated roster, are the additions to the church during the past three or five years. By consulting the pastor and others in the church who may know the newcomers, divide the additions into biological, conversion, and transfer categories.

2. Ways out of the church. Those persons listed in the dated roster, but unlisted in the current one, are the losses that occurred during the previous three or five years. Consult the persons who may know them and categorize them into death, reversion, and transfer headings.

> For further information on charting the ways into and out of the church, refer to Vergil Gerber, *A Manual for Evangelism/Church Growth,* pp. 52-55.

C. Distance distribution. In order to discover how far the members live from the church or from each other, find a map of the city in which the church is located and pinpoint the residence of each member on it. Observe the patterns of the geographical distribution. Do most members live within a three-mile radius? Do they live in clusters or are they widely dispersed? Where do they come from? From the better residential areas? From the government housing projects?

D. Ask the local pastor the following questions related to Christian conviction and evangelistic fervor.

   1. What ways of evangelism do you find most effective?

   2. Do you have ardent laymen who win people to Christ? Any program for training such?

   3. Is any young man training for the ministry from this church?

   4. What is your expectation for membership growth three, five, or ten years from now?

   5. Do Christian leaders in this church believe that

     ____ theirs is the only church (or denomination) which leads to salvation? (insert yes or no.)

     ____ all religions are various ways to the same God?

     ____ the era of sending missionaries overseas is over?

     ____ the primary task of the church is not to convert men to Christ but to humanize the world through social action?

IV. Give your suggestions for future membership growth of Church X.

PART III

HOW CHURCHES GROW

Because of the rigorous church growth research conducted especially during the past two decades, the Christian world mission knows much about the various ways in which the church does and does not grow. Much more is yet to be known. Chapters 5 and 6 deal with cases which will illustrate some of these known causes of growth and obstruction. Only by applying the methods which God has blessed to multiply His disciples does the church grow. Church leaders of America should master a number of church growth case studies now available, like the examples to follow, in order to see whether the principles of growth delineated in them are actually applicable to their situations in America.

Chapter 5
PATTERNS OF RAPID GROWTH

Four units, each a case study of rapid church growth, make up this chapter. The prominent factors which affect church growth are seen in actual cases from Brazil, Japan, North America, and Peru. In each case, numerous causes are given to explain the growth achieved. A combination of factors in proper proportion produces the many varieties of church growth. This combination varies from church to church; yet, there are some common factors which generally contribute to rapid growth. The eleven lessons drawn from the four case studies are among the most important of such ingredients.

22: THE *CONGREGAÇÃO CRISTA* IN BRAZIL

Convinced of the Lord's call and out of their desire to evangelize their ethnic families in mother tongue, two men of Italian descent left their homes in Chicago for Argentina in 1909. Feeling led by the Holy Spirit they continued their journey to São Paulo, Brazil. Shortly they discovered the unfruitfulness of their labor there and one returned to Argentina while the other, Louis Francescon, decided to remain and visit Platina, in the state of Paraná, responding to an earlier request made by an Italian. Francescon left behind a congregation in Platina when he returned to São Paulo in June, 1910. William Read describes what happened there.

> Francescon . . . was invited to stay in the home of Philip Pavin, Rua Alfandega, in the district of the Bras. There was a Presbyterian Church functioning in this district, and one Sunday Louis was given an opportunity to preach in it. He spoke in Italian. One of the Presbyterian elders disagreed violently with the manner and message and ordered Sr. Louis out of the Church. As Louis Francescon left the Presbyterian group, others went with him, which led eventually to the splitting of this Presbyterian Church which was just getting started in the area. Some members of the Congregação believed that the Lord sent their founder, Louis Francescon, into the Presbyterian Church to "straighten them up" and call out a great number to the glory and honor of His name, but the Presbyterians would not listen. The result today: the Presbyterian Church in the Brás numbers a few hundred while the Congregação Cristã in Brazil numbers thousands.[1]

The growth of the *Congregação* has been remarkable. It grew from zero in 1910 to 264,020 communicants in 1962. Its strength lies in the capital and states of São Paulo and Paraná. The total number of baptisms in 1962 alone was 23,809 and fifty-three percent of the baptisms came from the state and city of São Paulo. Thirty percent came from the state of Paraná. Of 1,770 church buildings, 777 were owned and 993 rented in 1962.[2] No overseas funds were spent to build these churches. Since there are no paid workers, whatever was given to the church treasury has been used to erect new church buildings. The *anciãos* (unpaid ministers) are highly respected and nine of them constitute a commission equivalent to a presbytery to handle district affairs. Regarding inter-church relations, the *Congregação* does not associate with other churches. This arises out of the conviction that there is no salvation outside the *Congregação*.

Why did the *Congregação* grow as it did? Several reasons are suggested, as follows:

This church got its start among the Italians who swarmed into Brazil during the closing decades of the nineteenth century. São Paulo State had developed a program which brought in tens of thousands to man their . . . farms . . . In 1950 the city and country of São Paulo contained 24 percent of the state's population, and of this population, 316,589 or 46 percent was the foreign-born element. Italians constitute a majority of the foreign-born element.

When the founder, Louis Francescon, an Italian himself, arrived in Brazil, he had ready entry into a huge Italian colony. He preached, lived, worked, pastored, and baptized in this Italian element. He had no cultural barriers to overcome. The movement spread among the Italians, and, as the years passed, it jumped naturally and progressively from the Italian to the Brazilian without any difficulty, for by 1930 two generations of Italians had integrated successfully into the Brazilian society and the founder had begun to preach and teach in Portuguese instead of Italian. . . .

[São Paulo] was the promised land for uprooted Brazilians from many of the northern states. Hundreds of thousands came in waves seeking a new start and opportunity. They had left behind their families and religious ties, and Roman Catholic priests did not know them. They were not averse to religious change. The Congregação was in an ideal position to take advantage of the ingress of these receptive multitudes. When it switched from Italian to Portuguese (about 1935) it evangelized and baptized tens of thousands of migrants from the interiors of the states. The original Congregação grew rapidly in this environment. Then it grew more when some of the converted northerners returned to their former homes, telling the good news, urging family and friends to join them, and starting new churches in Minas Gerais, Mato Grosso, Bahia, and Goiás. . . .

This young Church put no hindrances in the way of the new converts. No conditions beyond confessing the Lord have to be met for baptism, except that couples be already married according to civil law. Many have been welcomed into fellowship without any preparation period. Only after becoming baptized members did they learn the responsibilities of their new relationship in the Congregacão and what their "obedience" really meant. . . .

This young Church is not troubled by institutions, financial subsidies, pastoral support, or church policies that limit its activities in any way. Instead, it has one aim and goal, to be humble before the Lord, not allowing anything to hinder liberty of action in evangelizing and baptizing men in the name of the Father, Son, and Holy Spirit. Having this singleness of purpose contributes to success in church extension. . . .

A certain mentality has grown up around the prophecy of their founder that the Church has a divinely inspired "particular" mission to fulfill. Members think of the Congregação as an agency of the Lord at a particular time and place in the work of harvesting. . . . Many in the Congregação believe this prophecy is especially for them and is being fulfilled in a greater measure every year as the number baptized soars astronomically. This has a psychological effect upon the whole Church. It creates an atmosphere of expectancy. It aids growth and progress. . . .

Each member is taught to feel his missionary responsibility. As new members are baptized, they begin to learn what their new relationship is to God and to their fellow man. Every 15 days they have special services at which they "tarry" for the promise of the Holy Spirit. All are urged to move toward this experience with the Holy Spirit. In the process, new members are integrated into the missionary community and activity of the Congregação . . . the members pray, work, testify, sing, have fellowship, and evangelize with fiery zeal.[3]

* * * * *

Lesson 1: The Intensity of Belief and Church Growth

The *Congregação* makes an exclusive claim that it is the sole carrier of salvation. Nowhere else can one find salvation except in the *Congregação.* Such intense belief in the rightness of one's church is often related to the growth of a church. McGavran, after making extensive studies of church growth in Afericasia, concludes: "There is a definite relationship between the intensity of belief, often expressed in absoluteness and exclusiveness, and the rate of growth."[4]

Lesson 2: The People Movement and Church Growth

The *Congregação* arose out of an Italian people movement. A dedicated Christian of Italian descent from Chicago preached the gospel in Italian to Italian immigrants in Brazil and a fast growing | *Refer to Unit 17 for the basic concept of people movement.* |

church emerged. Since the days of the New Testament, the rapid growth of the church has been characterized by the spread of the gospel through web relationships within a particular segment of society. For example:

At the time of Christ the Jews had a very highly developed people-consciousness. They were full of "race prejudice." They thought of themselves not merely as a people, but as the People of God, the Chosen People. They strictly forbade any intermarriage with Gentiles. They had "no dealings with Samaritans," even though the latter were a kindred people. They were as caste-conscious as are the castes of India to-day. It is essential to realize that, when the Christian

Movement started to grow on the day of Pentecost, it was a movement of these people-conscious Jews only. The Lord Jesus Christ was thought of as a Jewish figure. He had lived as a Jew. The early Church was made up of Jews only. It was a one-people Church for some years. It could have been nothing else. . . .

This People Movement among the Jews spread rapidly among relatives. It was not confined rigorously to them, as the case of the Ethiopian eunuch and other instances show, but from the day that Andrew found his brother onward, those became Christian who already had family members in the fold.[5]

—Donald McGavran
The Bridges of God

The people movement is not confined only to a closed, tight-knit society inhabited by persons of high people-consciousness. The wave of rapid industrialization will eventually loosen such a society and the traditional family structure becomes more atomized. Yet despite such atomization, the web of family relationship has not lost its cohesive power, especially in Africasia. In fact, a recent report from rapidly industrialized Brazil accentuates the importance of considering the web as "one of the promising factors as regards the possibilities for church growth."

* * * * *

Diagram the family tree from the following description and trace the spread of the gospel.

One evening out of curiosity Sr. Gregorio entered the Methodist Church. He liked what he heard and began to attend regularly. Soon he believed, made his profession of faith, and was baptized.

Dona Ivani, his wife, along with the children, began to participate in the life of the church. Six months later she was baptized and joined the church.

An adolescent son, Robison, became interested in the Gospel, made a decision for Christ, and is in preparation for baptism.

The relationship web included another community, Vila Oeste, where Sr. Gregorio's mother-in-law lived. Motivated by the changed lives of her daughter's family, she came over weekly to attend their church, made her profession of faith, and was baptized.

About a year later the uncle of Gregorio's wife (brother of the mother-in-law), influenced by the experience of his sister, began to attend the services. Soon he too believed and became a member of the church. Two brothers of Dona Ivani in Vila Oeste have recently begun attending services.[6]

—Leon Strunk
from *Church Growth Bulletin*

* * * * *

A question may be asked as to the relationship of the people movement to church growth. In what way does the people movement aid church growth? What are the advantages of the people-movement way into the church as contrasted to the one-by-one pattern of accession creating a church made up largely of individuals extracted from their families? We suggest three advantages:

1. People-movement growth prevents the social dislocation of converts because a significant number within a homogeneous unit turn to Christ at the same time. The church has a better chance of maintaining the converts intact spiritually and socially. Membership leakage due to spiritual and social starvation caused by social dislocation is kept minimal.

2. People-movement growth enables the converts to keep alive the contacts with their non-Christian relatives. Membership growth takes place only when non-Christians are converted to Christ. Any church without ready access to the non-Christian population is headed for stagnation. Sometimes the relatives turn against their Christian kin. However, the actual cases of great growth prove that such growth is dependent on the pattern of *"multi-individual, mutually interdependent* conversion."

3. People-movement growth produces congregations which are more self-efficient and indigenous in handling finance, leadership, and discipline. People-movement congregations are less reliant on mission for support. Natural leaders are born within the group. The matters of discipline are handled by the nationals themselves and therefore without the stigma of foreignness. Self-propagating and readily reproducible congregations come into being from the people-movement pattern of growth.

Lesson 3: Social Structure, Receptivity, and Church Growth

Each society has a structure of its own and responds uniquely to the gospel. A society may be totalitarian or democratic, largely rural or largely urban, tightly closed with high people-consciousness or freely open with low people-consciousness. It may lie on either end of the class-mass societal axis or somewhere in between. Further, within each society, there are sub-societies made up of varieties of people. Some are landowners with power; others are tenants and without power. One segment of the population may speak Spanish as a primary language, while the rest of the population uses English. It is crucial for church growth to recognize the reality of social structure beyond mere surface appearances and to assess the degree of receptivity toward the gospel.

The *Congregação* grew most expansively in São Paulo, which was on the road to becoming a melting-pot community. There uprooted Brazilians came from the north seeking a new start. The traditional hold of Roman Catholicism was on the wane, and the people were more open to religious change. The church is bound to grow when it concentrates its evangelistic effort on a receptive population, whether receptiveness is caused by an erosion of belief in the traditional religion, a conquest of a nation by another, a contact of a culture with another, nationalism, or revolution.

Against the backdrop of a rapidly changing society, the *Congregação* saw its original growth exclusively among people of Italian descent, though after a quarter of a century it also began to penetrate heavily among Portuguese-speaking Brazilians in São Paulo and through them to other states. Francescon at first concentrated on his own people who, being recent immigrants, had faced many changes with much anxiety. The seed of the gospel fell on a fertile ground and grew.

Identifying the receptivity of a particular stratum within a society is a key to effective evangelism. Wayne Long of Dallas, Texas, reports on the receptivity of Cuban immigrants to the gospel. Dallas is one of America's large cities. To a casual observer the city appears to have one face (Americans), while in fact many faces are represented. Pastor Long sees in the city a population composed of Anglo-Americans, Mexican-Americans, Cuban-Americans, Indian-Americans, and Black-Americans. In the eastern section of Dallas where his church is located, he comes into daily contact with such varieties of people. He has commented that "there is an openness to Evangelical Christianity among these Cuban-Americans, especially the most recent arrivals." Many of the recent Cuban immigrants are professionals with a high level of education. "The leadership is there," he observes. Church growth principles should be applied to reach fifteen hundred Cubans in the city of Dallas and six hundred more in the county. It is reported that these persons are not worshiping in significant numbers in either Roman Catholic or Protestant churches. They are strangers in a new land trying to adjust themselves. Many of them cannot speak English. House churches are being planted with Cuban leaders in charge under the guidance of

Pastor Long, who handles Spanish well. More experiments of this kind should be conducted in the cities of the "nation of immigrants."

Lesson 4: Post-Baptismal Instruction and Mobilizing the Laity

The *Congregação* has no prolonged pre-baptismal instruction. Only the confession of Christ's lordship is required for church membership. One learns of Christian responsibilities, the meaning of obedience. and other teachings after baptism. The way of the *Congregação* has much advantage for church growth. The original enthusiasm of a new convert is not lost by a long period of waiting. Baptism marks the beginning—and not the end—of an adventure with Christ. What is more essential is a well-developed system of post-baptismal instruction so that each convert is equipped with basic Christian teachings and feels challenged to persuade others to Christ. Especially where there is great growth, the care of the flock after baptism is unavoidable for nurturing the on-going movement or even for preventing a large number of dropouts from the faith. The growth momentum must be carefully preserved and can be preserved by mobilizing the entire membership. Strachan says: *"The expansion of any movement is in direct proportion to its success in mobilizing its total membership in continuous propagation of its beliefs."*[7] The doctrine of the priesthood of all believers must be put into practice.

Lesson 5: Policy and Church Growth

Church growth is either advanced or impeded by mission/church policies. The *Congregação* has held a single, clearly defined goal of church planting. Policies related to institutions, financial support, and leadership were shaped to further the chief aim of reconciling men to God.

The church or mission in Africasia invariably finds itself in the midst of myriad human needs and offers services to meet them with a varying degree of commitment. Those who experience God's love can do no less than to share it with others by feeding the hungry, clothing the naked, healing the sick, and championing the oppressed. Yet, however great these needs may be, the church must not delude itself into thinking that the humanizing activities are the sole and primary task entrusted to it. On the contrary, human needs are to be met more effectively by the *increase* of individuals who are compelled to love and aid their neighbors because of their awareness of God's love for them. The church's central task is no other than to bring men and women into the saving and redemptive relationship in order that they might be new creatures in Christ. The church which considers social action as its primary policy, de-emphasizing evangelism and church planting, grows more slowly than the one which stresses the policy of persuading men to become Christ's followers and responsible members of His church.

Lesson 6: The Psychology of Expectancy for Greater Growth

The members of the *Congregação* firmly believed in the prophecy of their founder that their church was divinely commissioned for the task of harvesting. Evangelism-centered activities were carried out in obedience to the founder's prophecy. The membership grew right before their eyes year after year. The conviction that the prophecy was being fulfilled became stronger. Expectancy for greater growth developed and evangelistic efforts increased. Success generated enthusiasm. There is a definite relationship between expecting great things and attempting great things. And the satisfaction of expectation becomes a fuel for further activities.

Lesson 7: The Holy Spirit and Church Growth

The church growth movement, quite contrary to the opinions of some of its critics, places heavy emphasis upon the role of the Holy Spirit. After all, the church on the Day of Pentecost came into being by the unleashing of the Holy Spirit, and the Holy Spirit has been the energizing force behind the Christian world mission ever since.

The experience of the Holy Spirit is one of the central doctrines of the *Congregação* and the members are constantly urged to move toward this experience. In time, the new converts are incorporated into the missionary activities of the church and they proclaim the gospel with fiery zeal. The Holy Spirit is very much present when a person is converted to Jesus Christ and when nominal Christians are revived in their faith and lifted to a new height in their devotion to Christ and their understanding of His teachings. The Holy Spirit sends forth those renewed and revitalized Christians as witnesses to the redemptive act of Christ. All those to whom these witnesses are sent do not have the same degree of receptivity to the gospel. Some fields are ripe for a harvest while others are not. It is the Holy Spirit who cultivates the hearts of men and we are but to identify those sectors of the world which He has prepared for harvesting. In this respect, the church growth strategy of "winning the winnable" takes on an added meaning. The church generally grows when the Spirit-filled men zealously proclaim the gospel to those in the responsive stratum of society which God has cultivated and blessed.

Lesson 8: The Dynamics of Individual Witnesses

The *Congregação* was born because of the dynamic witness of Francescon. The cases of great growth are often associated with the dynamics of individual witnesses. They may be missionaries, pastors, or laymen. For example, Tippett refers to the story of the Chief of Atua who, after hearing John Williams' sermon, became converted. His testimony won his own and two other islands in rapid succession. "This was part of a mighty tide," says Tippett, "that swept the Pacific from island to island in a few years—15,000 in Tahiti, 11,000 in the Hervey Islands, 33,000 in Samoa—100,000 Polynesians in thirty years in the islands and another 70,000 in New Zealand in the same period. 30,000 in Tonga in three years, overflowing into Fiji for 100,000, overflowing again into New Britain and New Ireland for another 100,000, and again into Papua and then into the Solomons. No one can read the documents and say this was a matter of mere numbers—the Spirit of God was certainly in it."[8]

Another remarkable story comes from Formosa between 1939 and 1945. McGavran writes:

> The Highlanders of Formosa are a tough Malayan people. Living in inaccessible mountain fastnesses for centuries they maintained their independence from Chinese and Japanese conquerors. In 1925 they were finally subdued by the Japanese. Scattered schools among them taught some of them to read in Japanese. Practically none had become Christians.
>
> Then about 1930 a lone woman was converted and became a Bible-woman. About 1938 her teaching began to rouse interest in one small section of one small clan. As the coming World War began to influence action, the Japanese forbade this teaching of Christianity. Bible-woman Chi-o-ang could no longer go to interested villages. So those who wanted instruction came to her—at night. They purchased Bibles in Japanese. They started teaching others. In an effort to stamp out "this subversive sect" the Japanese beat, imprisoned, starved, and killed leaders, raided villages for Bibles, and harried the seekers. But secret Bible-study continued in fields and forests and midnight meetings. At the end of the war over 4,000 clansmen came down out of the hills asking for baptism. This started a great discipling which in the last ten years has brought over 50,000 into the Church and is still going on.[9]

Still another example comes from Tabasco, Mexico. Bennett describes it as follows:

> An illiterate baker sold his "two kinds of bread" from door to door. He could turn quickly to key passages underlined in his Bible and hand it to the listener to read. He left several semi-organized congregations in his wake.[10]

There are many such stories, including the case of Francescon. Church growth will be greatly advanced if the most effective of these witnesses are chosen and their methods of discipling analyzed and copied.

23: THE DOSHISHA AND HOLINESS CHURCH REVIVALS

Much misunderstanding exists on the subject of revival. What is revival? What is the relationship of revival to church growth? Why do some revivals lead to much church growth while others do not? What are the factors which make the difference? Read the following selection with these questions in mind.

A comparative study of the Doshisha and Holiness church revivals in prewar Japan illumines the relationship of revival to church growth relevant to the Christian World Mission today.

Frequent entries are made in the annals of Japanese church history that a series of revivals followed the missionary and national Christian conventions of 1883 and that many Christians were revived and through them others came to accept the faith. Uncritical reading of historical documents about the revivals of the 1880's might incline the reader to reach an erroneous conclusion that the great growth of the 1880's enjoyed by some major Protestant denominations was singularly caused by the revivals. One gets such an impression by going over the narratives and accounts of some individual cases. It is true that in the period between 1882 and 1889, Congregational and Presbyterian Churches made extremely rapid gains—the Congregational Church from 1,000 to 9,000, and the Presbyterian Church from 2,000 to slightly less than 9,000. The former multiplied by nine—increased over 900 per cent—and the latter by 4.5—450 per cent—in less than ten years. The Methodist Church which was on equal footing with the Congregational Church in 1882 advanced in this period, but not as greatly.

More careful reading of the documents, however, helps us correct this error. The facts are as follows. The "fires of spiritual 'revival' began to burn among the foreign community in Yokohama in 1883."[11] They spread first to some of the girls' schools in the city and then to the Methodist-related Aoyama Gakuin in Tokyo. The flames of spiritual fires spilled over other places such as Kyoto, Sendai, Nagoya, Nagasaki, and Oita in Kyushu.[12] In each place, a small group of young Christians became spiritually vivified and those influenced by them professed their faith. "One of the most marked of these," wrote Cary, "was in the Doshisha."[13] It is reported [14] that several Christian students met in a daily meeting about the first of March, 1884. By March 16, the whole school, as the story goes, was influenced by this spiritual surge. But school authorities, especially the missionaries, tried to prevent the students from becoming extravagant in their behavior by urging

> as strongly as they knew how, that the regularity of school life
> be maintained as regards studies, meals, exercise, and sleep;

that the prayer-meetings be held early in the evening and be rigidly restricted to one hour; and that special pains be taken to secure quiet during the evening.[15]

So the result was that, after some two hundred students were baptized,[16] things returned to normal.

In other words, the Doshisha revival and the revivals of the 1880's in general took place in schools at different times each lasting for a short duration and did not develop into a spiritual combustion sweeping the entire nation in one big blaze. "Revival" meant in those days a gracious blessing of God's spirit, sweeping churches and schools and leading many in both communities to deeper dedication and also to new and more open commitment to Christ. Revival did trigger some conversions—among sodalities of students, but was confined to the schools. It was therefore unable to spread to families for students, residing in dormitories, were not in living contact with their families.

The Holiness Church, an indigenous Christian movement founded in Japan by Jyuji Nakada in 1905, experienced the revivals of a different kind in the 1930's—those that actually resulted in great ingathering.

The people believing in the "pure gospel" preached revival, expected revival, and put their faith in revival. The revival for which these people were waiting finally began to take place at Yodobashi Holiness Church in Tokyo toward the end of November, 1919. Though it spread to various churches in the city, this revival was confined to the vivification of the pastors and members without the conversions of non-Christians into the faith and thus without greater growth in the membership. Commenting on the results of the revival of 1919-20, Nakada listed the following four items: (1) the qualitative development of the membership; (2) an increase in giving; (3) the spiritual unity with men of other denominations (mostly pastors) who shared in the revival meetings; (4) an increase in the spirit of evangelism.[17]

On May 19, 1930 there occurred another revival, [18] this time, at the Tokyo Bible Seminary where students had been earnestly praying for revival. When suddenly the prayer meeting turned into one of intensity and excitement, some students recognized this to be the revival and rushed to the homes of their professors with the news. They too joined the meeting and prayed shoulder to shoulder in loud voices. There were some who even began dancing.

They continued to pray. When Nakada returned to Tokyo from his trip to Korea and Manchuria, he encouraged the Holiness churches in Tokyo to hold prayer meetings from May 30 through June 7. And on June 8, a Pentecostal meeting was held at the seminary. For the next two and a half years, various revival meetings of both large and small scale were held in many different cities in Japan. The leaders of the Holiness Church traveled extensively, preached often, and prayed intensely.

Thus, by the end of 1930, the Holiness Church had an accession of 4,311 reaching the total membership of 12,046. At the end of the following year, there were 3,487 conversions. The growth continued till 1932 when the membership numbered 19,523.

In both cases, revival meant revitalization of existing Christians—those whose allegiance was already in Christ but lacked vitality. This was accomplished by incessant Bible study, intense prayer, and descent of the Holy Spirit. The outcome was vital Christian living and unequivocal desire to share the good news.

What made the difference between the two cases was that one took place among the Christians who were not in living contact with their families and relatives whose allegiance was not yet in Christ and the other occurred among those who were.

Furthermore, the way the revival was "handled" made the difference. In the Doshisha revival, school authorities, especially the missionaries brought up in the tradition of the Eurican Church, resisted the unleashing of spiritual energy through cautious measures. In the 1919 Holiness revival, leaders, while having prayed for revival earnestly and patiently, were unable to nurture it when it came. The story of the 1930 revival is told differently, however. The experience of the earlier revival and Nakada's leadership helped fan the spiritual fires beyond the walls of Tokyo across the entire country holding meetings in various Holiness churches. These revival meetings of both large and small scale deepened the spiritual life of the whole Holiness constituency and heightened its evangelistic zeal. And the members, in living contact with a non-Christian population, brought men and women into the faith.[19]

—Tetsunao Yamamori
from *Church Growth Bulletin*

* * * * *

Lesson 9: Revival and Church Growth

Understanding revival and its dynamics is essential to church growth. There is a variety of revivals. The comparative study of different types of revival illumines the relationship of revival to the growth process. This case study is one such example. On the basis of the above article some general comments can be made regarding that relationship.

Revival means revitalization of existing Christians and does not by itself bring about church

Revival bears a close relationship to church growth; yet exactly what that relationship is, particularly in Africasia where the Church is growing on new ground, is often not clear. Under certain conditions revival may be said to cause growth. Under others, its relationship to church is so distant that apparently revival occurs without growth and growth without revival.[20]

—Donald McGavran
Understanding Church Growth

growth. Under certain circumstances it issues in growth, but under others it does not.

Revival is initiated by incessant Bible study, intense prayer, and the power of the Holy Spirit. And it blossoms into great growth only where there is expectation for, faith in, and importance attached to revival. Once it occurs, revival must be nurtured and developed with great care by the persons aware of the dynamics of revival before great church growth occurs. For instance, the Doshisha revival was not only mishandled but there was no such expectation by school authorities. Further, the Holiness revival died of insufficient knowledge on the part of the leaders. The later one was a different story.

Revival grows rapidly when the revitalized Christians are in living contact with their non-Christian families and relatives. The Doshisha revival was sealed off from potential growth because the students were in the school dormitories away from home.

The second Holiness revival grew tremendously because it occurred within an indigenous church movement. Nakada, along with his lieutenants, traveled extensively throughout the country and fanned the revival fire to reach the relatives and friends of the now vivified members of various congregations. Obviously, revival heightened the evangelistic zeal of the entire Holiness constituency and growth followed.

24: THE OAK LANE STORY

The decline of membership of a once wealthy and influential urban congregation is not new in a modern America whose cities have grown and changed rapidly in the past few decades. Oak Lane Presbyterian Church in Philadelphia, Pennsylvania, is no exception. It had been on the decline in its membership for the previous twenty years when, in the fall of 1957, some sixty concerned members met to discuss the future of their church. The Oak Lane story tells about the renewal of a city church and serves as a case study for urban church growth. Following is the pastor's narrative of the church's experience.

* * * * *

It began with a series of sermons on evangelism, backed up by articles in the church magazine, letters to the congregation, and many discussions with individuals and groups. First the session [the ruling body of a Presbyterian congregation, consisting of the elders] had to be convinced, because I knew there wasn't likely to be any evangelistic action without their support. . . .

I shared my conviction with the session that every local church should be mission-minded and evangelistically oriented. Evangelism is not to be thought of as a program which a church adopts for a time. Rather it is part of the mission of the church to be evangelistic. Visitation evangelism is simply the procedure through which a church carries out its evangelistic function and expresses its evangelical concern. It is the Christian education function of the church to help those who are brought into the church to grow in their faith and understanding and to express it in meaningful action in the church, in the community, and beyond. The session agreed and Operation Doorbell was given the green light. A major congregational dinner was held with a carefully planned program designed to inform, inspire, and enlist those present in Operation Doorbell. . . .

Those who had agreed to be callers attended a series of training sessions designed to develop confidence and competence through role playing, questions and answers, and other means. Some helpful background materials were distributed, including pamphlets which explained the Biblical and theological basis for evangelism, the nature and purpose of witnessing, and how to make an evangelistic call, with suggested responses to typical excuses.

We had also prepared some materials for the visitors to leave with those upon whom they called. These included a pamphlet for prospective members, entitled "How to Join the Church," a sheet outlining the various services which the church offered the community; the booklet describing the history and program of the church; the church bulletin, which is the best calling card; copies of the monthly church magazine; and other specialized literature, such as flyers announcing coming events . . . After reviewing the church calendar for the year, the Membership Committee arbitrarily chose Monday as the night when there were the fewest activities to interfere. . . .

A deliberate effort was made to limit the total time consumed each Monday night to about two and one-half hours. The format was fairly standard. Callers were asked to be at the church by 7:30 P.M. for briefing and assignments. I would assist Mr. Prentice in assigning the calling partners and distributing the cards to each team, giving any specific instructions or information that might be helpful to the callers. Newcomers were teamed with experienced callers. In the beginning there was always a short training session, during which I would discuss some aspect of evangelism or witnessing. As time went by, my remarks dealt more with specific situations and problems we had encountered.

The briefing session lasted no more than fifteen minutes, at the conclusion of which someone would be asked to lead us in prayer. The callers were also urged to have a brief word of prayer with their teammate before each visit, asking God to prepare the way and to guide them in their conversion. At 7:45 the callers would depart two by two, hopefully a man and woman together, although there was not always an even distribution between the sexes. The teams were instructed not to ring any doorbells after 9:00 P.M. and to return to the church as soon after that as possible.

Upon returning each team would spend a few minutes entering the appropriate information on their cards, initialing and dating their entries for future reference. When the majority had arrived, we would gather at tables for what was for all of us both literally and figuratively "the icing on the cake." A dedicated kitchen crew would serve light refreshments, as the teams reported the results of their calls. It was a wonderful time of fellowship, always instructive and inspiring, as the callers shared their experiences and offered comments to one another.

This was the heart of our on-going training program. We learned from one another how to tackle most any kind of situation, from how to talk with a television set blaring away and how to cope with an over-friendly mutt that thinks he's a lap dog and isn't, to what you say to a nuclear physicist who cordially informs you he is an atheist or to a distraught widow whose husband has just died of cancer. We came to know our community well and the people who lived in it. There were hundreds of human dramas unfolding behind the doors whose bells we rang, and we became part of them. . . .

Sometime between 9:30 and 10:00 o'clock we'd be ready for our closing prayer, and there was always much for which to thank God. If one team had a discouraging night, another would be jubilant. There was always something good to report, and even those who had met with no positive response knew that they had at least sown some seeds which could bear fruit some day. We never failed to ask God's continued blessing on those who had been visited, especially those who might have been wrestling with a decision of faith or who had some special need.

That, in brief, was the format of a typical Monday night. . . .

Within three months we had reversed the downward membership trend, having recouped the losses that had occurred over the first eight months of that year. Twenty-nine persons were received into the membership of the church in November, and from that time on there was a new class every three months. In a little more than four years we received 253 new members, as our membership climbed to more than 500.

All the while we were engaged in a systematic "roll-cleaning" effort, encouraging our nonresident members to affiliate with churches where they were presently living and restimulating the interest of those who were backsliding within our own parish. In the same four-year period we issued Letters of Transfer for 85 persons and suspended 54 more, all of the latter group having been inactive for at least four years.[21]

—Richard S. Armstrong
The Oak Lane Story

* * * * *

Lesson 10: Urbanization and Church Growth

Urbanization, the migration of people to the city, has accompanied the industrial development around the globe and is one of the most significant phenomena of the twentieth century. Greenway speaks of its impact upon the Christian mission as follows:

At the beginning of the twentieth century only about 13 percent of the world's population lived in the cities and 87 percent in rural areas. But by the end of the century the situation will be completely reversed. By then 87 percent of all people will reside in urban areas. Obviously the rural-orientated missionary patterns of past decades will be largely obsolete in the years ahead.[22]

Urban migrants are the newcomers to the city and often experience drastic reorientation in their lives. Unlike the rural community, urban life is impersonal. The long-cherished values of the country life are suddenly challenged by the mores of the city. During the transition period, urban migrants are lonely because they have been uprooted from the close-knit family and friendship ties and thrown into the impersonal world of systems. They are in varying degrees frustrated in coping with the new world. They are at the same time open to new ideas and new ventures. For some, the anonymity of the city is a threat, but for others, it serves as the basis for new experiments, being freed for the first time from many of the restrictions of the traditional society. In this context, many in fact become receptive to the gospel. Urbanization is one of those external forces which aid church growth, provided that effective methods are employed to harness this potential.

Unfortunately, the discipling of the cities in Africasia has been rather limited. In America, all denominations are extremely concerned about the urban setting of the church. Millions of dollars have been spent since 1950 to explore experimental ministries. And yet reports in this area are alarming. Many experiments remain at the level of exploration and are being conducted in the dark. A large number have been diverted from their original churchly concerns. They do not have strategies to propose to local churches surrounded by apartment houses and changing neighborhoods. Books upon books with urban concerns are published, but hardly any book gives clear guidance as to the effective ways to multiply churches in urban America. The churches in the cities may not be like the present churches. They may indeed be Christian cells. How can multiplying Christian cells be planted in high-rise apartments and changing urban neighborhoods, among city-migrated, city-born, and city-bred persons? This is precisely the question that needs to be answered by any churchly experiment in the city. The method of visitation evangelism described in the Oak Lane Story is only one among many methods. Urbanization is most rapid in America. What is now needed is a variety of case studies in numerous cities in America and across the world in order to develop definitive statements concerning urbanization and church growth.

Some guidelines are now known to further the multiplying of urban churches. They should be carefully studied and applied to specific situations.

Guidelines Suggested
by Donald McGavran:
1. Emphasize house churches.
2. Develop unpaid lay leaders.
3. Recognize resistant homogeneous units.

Guidelines Suggested
by Peter Wagner:
1. Discover the areas of fertile soil.
2. Set realistic goals.
3. Prepare to sacrifice.

4. Focus on the responsive.
5. Multiply tribe, caste, and language churches.
6. Surmount the property barrier.
7. Communicate intense belief in Christ.
8. Provide the theological base for an egalitarian society.[23]

4. Apply church growth principles.
5. Build follow-up into the program.
6. Be mobile and flexible.[24]

Based on your knowledge of urban churches in America, what guidelines and steps would you suggest for multiplying churches? What else could Oak Lane Presbyterian Church have done to enhance membership increase?

What sociological facts would you list as being important to understand the church's urban setting?

25: JOHN RITCHIE AND THE PERUVIAN CHURCH

John Ritchie arrived in Peru in 1906 from England. After devoting six months to Spanish study he accompanied a Bible Society colporteur on a journey through an isolated part of southern Peru. They traveled with a mule train carrying merchandise. They visited every house in each town and village offering the Scriptures for sale and reading Bible portions to the people. These years following the revolt in 1898 against the Spanish way of doing things were marked by a tremendous thirst for the printed word.

Ritchie observed that the buyer of a book frequently sat down at once and began to read aloud, and that the many who could not read gathered round and listened in silence. He further noticed that walls of houses were commonly papered with newspapers, and when muleteers were waiting for food to be prepared, one would go to the wall and begin reading the old papers. Others gathered round and listened. Ritchie became convinced that despite high illiteracy the way to evangelize the country was through the printed page.

The law at that time provided that periodicals printed in Peru should be mailed free to any address within the country. It was decided, therefore, to issue a monthly periodical rather than tracts. By October, 1911, a printer with suitable printing equipment had arrived from England and the first copy of *El Heraldo* was off the press.

New names and addresses were gathered from perusing the provincial daily press and other sources. Names were put on the mailing list for three issues and then dropped unless some response was forthcoming. The results of this circulation were surprising from the very first. Letters came from many places, including some to which the paper had not been sent by the publishers, asking for further issues, for books, for Bibles, and at times, for spiritual guidance. Contacts multiplied. Some wrote inviting John Ritchie to come and tell them more of the Gospel.

John Ritchie followed up contacts so far as possible. In each village he would be the guest of the person with whom he had been in correspondence. Most villagers quit work for the period of his visit. When they gathered to hear the message, he usually began by speaking of the lost sheep and the Good Shepherd, a theme familiar to them. But he did not attempt to conduct a regular church service with singing, prayer, sermon, and benediction. After his discourse, he stayed and awaited the inevitable questions.

He praised the first questioners for their discernment, so that everyone who could think up a question of his own hastened to propound it. So far as possible, he found some verse of Scripture and read it out of the Bible. On it he based his reply. Thus the Gospel was brought into the people's life. All the time there was being built up in them a desire to possess the Book which answered with such wisdom their deepest questions.

After a meal and some rest, proceedings would be resumed with another discourse, generally on sowing and reaping, which also was a subject with which they were familiar. Again, there would be questions and answers. From themes related to their daily life, the talks proceeded to those of sin and death, redemption through the blood of Christ, new birth through the operation of the Holy Spirit, and eternal life. So two or three days might be spent teaching whatever Ritchie felt the people could receive and use, not only of religious truth but also of Christian conduct, health and hygiene, arts and crafts, and improvements in their agricultural practices. He carried a homoeopathic medicine case, and, on occasion, ministered to the sick, selling nothing and taking no money, save only for books and periodicals. So a conviction was begotten in the people that Ritchie was interested in their welfare and sought nothing for himself.

Before the end of each such initial visit, the people invariably asked for a preacher or teacher so that they might have such services regularly. He told them that no such man was available and they did not need one. He encouraged them to come together each evening on returning from their fields, read a lesson from the Bible, and have prayer together. He suggested that on Sunday one who could read well might read something helpful from the tracts and papers that would be sent to them, or a sermon from a book which was available. Finally, he suggested that they name a small committee of those most interested, to make arrangements for these services, and to maintain correspondence with him. Later, churches grew out of such visits.

It is our surmise that Ritchie devised his plan for planting churches independently, but by 1915 he had become well acquainted with Roland Allen's writings, recognized his own procedures as basically Pauline in nature and began to use the full Pauline approach vigorously.

In 1918 delegates were gathered from churches to take counsel together. By 1920 annual meetings were duly organized, with two delegates from each local church. The first three days were devoted to business. The next three days were for all who would come and were devoted to the deepening of the spiritual life. The business sessions were called a Synod, the popular meetings a Convention. The delegates to the 1922 Synod numbered 19, representing 11 churches.

After the 1922 meeting, evangelistic activity burst out among the village churches. Several went to surrounding villages preaching, giving out *El Heraldo* and forming new worshiping congregations. In this way the movement spread over the region. Over one period of three years between 1922 and 1929 a new church was organized every month without interruption! By 1929 there were sixty organized churches—of perhaps 20 members each—meeting mostly in private homes. These were in various stages of growth, from the little gathering of seekers who had hardly begun to perceive the significance of their new-found faith and hope, up to the well-organized and ably-conducted church.

For better supervision, they were grouped into five districts or presbyteries, each with a paid Peruvian worker itinerating among its churches.

For their regular worship services, the local churches depended on their unpaid lay leaders.

These sixty churches were not dependent on foreign funds. The only big expense was the support of the five itinerating Peruvian workers. Ritchie made that an obligation of the presbyteries which they met from church offerings supplemented by incidental gifts from Christians in England. Ritchie gave the churches money boxes for the offering. These were always opened in view of the entire congregation and the amount entered in the book. Training was given in building and using a budget and being honest in the use of the Lord's resources.

When believers were first baptized in a village, the new church elected elders to hold office for a year. They were eligible for re-election.

Ritchie took no part in church discipline. He taught the congregations that the church was God's and theirs; each group was subject to the government of its own elders, and must learn to conduct its life under the guidance of the Holy Spirit and in the light of Holy Scripture. Ritchie taught high standards as essential to Christian discipleship. When they were violated, elders took such action as seemed proper to them after prayer, careful inquiry into the facts, and admonition of the delinquent. Their action usually leaned to severity rather than laxity.

The elders were encouraged to conduct the ordinary services, dedicate children, baptize believers, celebrate the Lord's Supper, conduct church marriage following civil ceremonies, and bury their dead with Christian rites. Much of the elder's work, Ritchie agreed, was primitive, but it had the advantages of being indigenous, free in its development, and commanding the devotion of truly awakened men and women who, though lacking much equipment, were interested in their service.

The churches established by Mr. Ritchie—later called the Iglesia Evangélica Peruana—numbered about seventy in 1930 with 1400 full members. They grew by spontaneous expansion among the villages of the Central Highlands of Peru. They differed markedly from the static little "churches" at most mission stations.[25]

—Keith E. Hamilton
Church Growth in the High Andes

* * * * *

Lesson 11: Indigenous Church Principles and Church Growth

In the above story, Hamilton well describes the indigenous method which Ritchie used in creating self-supporting, self-governing, and self-propagating congregations in Peru. In Latin America and elsewhere the evangelizing agencies which followed indigenous church principles have often obtained growth. Hamilton, after his careful study of church growth in the High Andes, enumerates seven such principles which have proven effective.

1. The Christian worker begins by broadcasting the gospel followed by regularly visiting earnest seekers, who are gathered into churches for instruction and fellowship.

2. The leadership of these churches should consist of unpaid men chosen from and selected by the local churches themselves.

3. Churches call paid pastors when they want them and are able to pay for them.

For the further elaboration of indigenous church principles, consult:
Roland Allen, *Missionary Methods: St. Paul's or Ours.*
Melvin Hodges, *The Indigenous Church.*
Jerry S. Key, *The Nevius Method of Carrying on Foreign Mission Endeavor.*
John Ritchie, *Indigenous Church Principles.*

4. Church buildings are to be constructed when the churches are ready and able to build them.

5. Church discipline is to be in the hands of the churches, using the rule of Scripture as the standard, constantly guided by the Holy Spirit.

6. Christian charity and mutual aid on the part of the churches should be carefully taught and practiced.

7. All financial arrangements made for the ordinary life and existence of the churches should be such that the people themselves can and will control and manage their own business independent of any foreign subsidy.[26]

There are both advantages and disadvantages to these evangelistic principles. The creation of an indigenous church is slow to develop and the process is often discouraging to the missionary. In the days of high-pressure advertising, a glorious report on a mission hospital, school, or orphanage produces more support from the home base than the creation of a solid indigenous church. Yet, advantages by far outstrip disadvantages. The indigenous church philosophy is anchored in Scripture, emphasizes church planting as the goal of mission, fosters a healthy, witnessing, and reproducible national church with little cost to the mission, and protects the Eurican churches from the charges of "Western Imperialism."

A question may be raised: Does the church growth school of thought advocate indigenous church principles at any cost? The answer is negative. Consider the following statement.

When establishing churches in resistant populations, try to start on indigenous church principles. The naturalness of these sometimes overcomes resistance. Do not, however, dully continue indigenous church principles for decades whether churches multiply or not. In a country like Nigeria or Brazil, a mission which with great indigenous church zeal has spent thirty years and two million dollars and has a total present membership of less than 400 baptized believers, is a poor steward of God's grace. It should have shifted to a limited subsidy plan, or otherwise adjusted its policies, many years ago. There is no merit in sticking to indigenous church principles whether churches are established or not. . . .

Make provision for paid leaders at the supervisory level. Sometimes direct payment from mission funds is necessary. It is no sin. It is not the best and most permanent arrangement, but it has produced good churches in hundreds of cases. Sometimes it is well to establish a church fund administered by the Church into which contributions from the congregations and the mission go, and from which workers and pastors are paid. The ultimate goal is for the national Church to pay local pastors, circle pastors and all other staff entirely from its own funds, but few Africasian Churches have yet reached the place where this goal is in sight.[27]

—Donald McGavran
Understanding Church Growth

Chapter 6
OBSTACLES TO RAPID GROWTH

Obstacles to rapid growth are numerous and varied. While many such obstacles are being discovered as a result of church growth research, no exhaustive list can be compiled. The factors obstructing growth also differ from one church to another and from one type of society to the next. In the final analysis, every churchman must learn to identify the true causes which stifle rapid growth in his region and among his people so that the strategies to correct these ills can be devised.

Unit 26 acquaints the reader with some known growth-arresting factors. This partial list of causes is useful only as a guide to investigation. Units 27—29 are actual cases of slow growth. They come from India, Mexico, and Africa. Obstructions to rapid growth vary in each case and must be examined individually. Read and analyze the selections and give answers to the questions at the end of each unit.

26: GROWTH ARRESTING FACTORS

The church in a given field may have never experienced growth of any significance from the beginning to the present. On the other hand, it may have enjoyed rapid growth for several years, but has suddenly reduced the growth rate, has gradually plateaued, or has sharply declined at a certain point. What causes such a phenomenon? A combination of factors generally explains it. The students of church growth should know some common reasons for lack of growth.

1. Leaders were chained to existent nonproductive work. Or, Church and mission were devoted to a nonproductive pattern, once needed but long since outmoded.

2. Church and mission were devoted to an only slightly productive pattern instead of a highly productive one. For example:
   They continued the school approach when adults could be won.
   They baptized no illiterates, though this limited the church largely to youth.
   They required a three-year catechumenate, though few adults could last the course.
   They tried to circumvent polygamy by baptizing chiefly unmarried youth and hoping they would stick to monogamy.

3. They did not learn the language of the people, worked always in English, and so established the image that the Christian religion signifies mainly cultural advance. They thus got a few of the rebel young men on their way out of the tribe, but very few older men of families.

4. Fearing the problems brought in by converts and churches made up of few Christians, they set very high standards and baptized few.

5. The ministry was too highly trained and paid, was not one with the people, and could not be supported by the churches themselves.

6. Church and mission allowed themselves to remain stuck in an area of low potential.

7. They "worked with" resistant homogeneous units, instead of baptizing the receptive units available to them:
   Roman Catholic ranchos instead of revolutionary ranchos
   Upper-class professional people instead of laborers
   High castes instead of depressed classes

High-school youth in towns instead of peasants in the country
The "classes" instead of the masses.

8. Leaders did not learn about church growth from mistakes of the past.
9. No one checked what was being done against the degree of church growth achieved.
10. The mission faced with little growth did not seek expert opinion from the outside.
11. They accepted gradualism as a sufficient mission method.

—Donald McGavran
Understanding Church Growth

> **Gradualism—the mission's engagement in good works now (such as Christian hospitals, schools, and literacy) in the hope that church growth may result later on.**

* * * * *

Review   1.

Chapter 5

carefully   2.

and

compose   3.

eleven

statements   4.

(one for

each   5.

lesson)

explaining   6.

the

circumstances   7.

under

which   8.

rapid

growth   9.

may

not   10.

occur.

Discuss   11.
the
validity
of each
statement.

* * * * *

Discuss the feasibility of today's strategy stated below.

The era has come when Christian Missions should hold lightly all mission station work, which cannot be proved to nurture growing churches, and should support the Christward movements within Peoples as long as they continue to grow at the rate of 50 per cent per decade or more. This is to-day's strategy.[2]

—Donald McGavran
The Bridges of God

27: THE GARAS AND THE MENNONITES

The Garas are a numerous oppressed-class people living in a territory extending from eastern Madhya Pradesh to the Bay of Bengal [in India]. The center of population lies in Orissa. In Madhya Pradesh the Garas are a scattered caste living in small groups of one to ten families. In Orissa they are the principal oppressed caste and live in groups of from five to seventy-five houses . . . Usually a part of their livelihood is earned by playing musical instruments and dancing at weddings, festivals, and the like. Where they comprise a large proportion of the population, they are also weavers, cultivators and village menials.

This is the people . . . in the midst of which an active Christian movement is found. It began in the English Baptist mission field of Sambhalpur about 1900 and spread west into Raigarh. . . .

Jagdishpur is a station of the General Conference Mennonite Mission, located near Basna in the Raipur District. Here exists another overflow of the Baptist Gara people movement. It started in 1916 through the efforts of one, Gopal by name, who having been baptized in Patna State migrated to a village near Basna. He was determined that his unconverted caste-fellows should hear the good news, and after unsuccessful attempts to bring help from Baptists and Evangelicals, enlisted the aid of the Mennonites. He was the moving spirit for several years and led hundreds to Christ. A converted man in the midst of his own approachable caste forty miles from a mission station was again the key to revival.

Ingathering continued till 1923. By that time about 750 people living in 42 villages in a territory ten by fifteen miles in extent had been baptized. In 1923 the people movement was arrested. Between 1923 and 1936 while the Baptist Church was growing from 8,000 to 15,000, the Mennonite Church of these same Gara people remained stationary at about 700. . . .

The causes leading to the arrest of this movement are so evident and so instructive for all Christians concerned in caste-wise revivals that we relate them, not to assess blame, but to illuminate the process by which Churches grow and decline.

At the outset, as was but natural at that time, there was an almost total lack of understanding of how the Church in India has grown, i.e. of how people movements have been developed into vigorous Churches. In the reports of 1924-34 there is no reference whatever to the fact that all the growth had taken place in one caste. Garas are mentioned, but not as the great open door, not as any more hopeful than the Gonds or the Aghariyas. No enumeration of the unconverted Garas was attempted. Indeed, because of the problems which the Gara converts brought with them into the Church, there was some tendency to regard these people as peculiarly difficult, and to question the value of more Garas in the Church. An able and vigorous evangelistic program was carried out but on an intercaste basis. The unit to be approached was the village, not a given caste. The sociological organism of the tribe or caste was believed to be of little importance in the jungle territory around Basna, a mistake often made by missions. Church evangelistic campaigns sent Christians out to witness to all alike, rather than to the unconverted amongst their own relatives and former caste-fellows. To sum it up, the open door was not recognized, and the Christian forces flung themselves against the granite walls.

The second cause for stoppage was the sudden change of regime. In the beginning the mission policy was one of granting generous privileges to Christians, of treating the new Christians in the same way as the older central station communities. Liberal aids to the education of the children and economic assistance of various sorts seemed reasonable. At the time of baptism a new sari or dhoti or a few annas were given to the convert. This policy was definitely altered in 1924 and many privileges were cut off. A goal was attempted which made for self-confidence and initiative. No transportation to children going to boarding school at Janjgir 60 miles away and at Mohidih 32 miles away was given. The pupils walked to and fro. No Christmas gifts were given to employees. The change from the one basis to the other basis is always difficult. In Basna it helped to stop growth.

Again, when a station was established at Jagdishpur in 1924, a large building program was necessary. Abundant work was provided for Christians. Poorer Christians moved to Jagdishpur and settled there. Although the larger number of the Christian community stayed in the villages and was not directly affected by this building program, nevertheless when, in addition to the changes indicated in the foregoing paragraphs, building work also ceased, Christians living in or near Jagdishpur tended to feel themselves ill treated, and the pressure fell upon the missionaries, who despite a policy which leaned the other way, felt that they really ought to do something to lift the economic status of the Christian community. A village school and dispensary were started. A "Weavers Association" was formed (these Garas are weavers by trade) to buy yarn and sell cloth co-operatively. This took a considerable share of time and attention. Jagdishpur and the nearby villages became a typical mission station with the bulk of the effort being inevitably spent on the Christian community. This care (medical, educational, and economic) tended to transform the Christians into people who considered themselves the beneficiaries of the Mission and to transform the Mission into an organization which considered its primary function that of caring for Christians.[3]

—J. W. Pickett
from *Church Growth and Group Conversion*

* * * * *

1. What basic church growth principles were violated in the arrested growth of the Mennonite church?

2. What would you have done to nourish the growth started by the efforts of Mr. Gopal?

28: THE PUZZLE PRESENTED BY MEXICO

The following graph presents the puzzle of the Evangelical Church in Mexico. The contrast between the great growth achieved by some sections of the Church and the limited growth of others is clearly apparent.

The lowest line on the graph represents the membership in Mexico of the Christian Church (Disciples of Christ), a large, aggressive North American Church with a highly organized foreign missions program. Though assisted most of the time by a dozen missionaries and considerable funds, the total membership has grown, declined, and grown again, from 485 in 1915 to 972 in 1960.

The next line represents the Southern Baptists, a vital, powerful Church in the United States with a vigorous foreign missions program. Mexico has been one of its major fields for over fifty years. Yet its Church, too, showed little growth until 1950. For forty years it plateaued at about 3000. Since 1950 it has grown steadily. See the upturn in the graph.

The top line shows a very different type of growth. It soars to 278,000 full members. Since these are accompanied by unbaptized believers and sympathizers, numbering possibly another 200,000, and the children of all three classifications, an Evangelical Community of possibly a million has been created in the last fifty years. Some Branches of the Church have been getting good growth. Some have not. . . .

The puzzle cannot be solved easily by invoking the myth of a "difficult land"—though the popularity of the myth is natural enough and some sections of Mexico are resistant to the missionary work of the Church. Some denominations, with great sacrifices and toil, established little bands of Evangelicals in cities, towns and villages; but these remained static worshiping groups of 20, 30, 40, or (at mission stations) of 80 to 200. In some villages lone families maintained the Evangelical spark for years. Inevitably, missionaries and Mexican ministers associated with these efforts have thought theirs "an Islamic land" where, because of the fanaticism of the population, their church really could not grow. Generations of missionaries, in mission after mission, have served in Mexico and seen only a few baptisms. Their church—they thought—did well to survive. It did "a good work." It "witnessed for Christ." It bore persecution bravely. It "served the people" through education, agriculture, and medicine. But it did not proliferate. The spark was there, but it lit no fire. . . .

Anyone who would understand church growth in Mexico must see . . . those elements, internal and external, which arrest the multiplication of churches. The external elements are intense Roman Catholic opposition and the chaos of war and revolution.

About the first, little needs to be said. The Roman Catholic Church stamped out the Reformation in Spain and resolved that Spanish possessions (Latin America and the Philippines) should be hermetically sealed against "the wicked and disastrous heresy." Protestants were literally

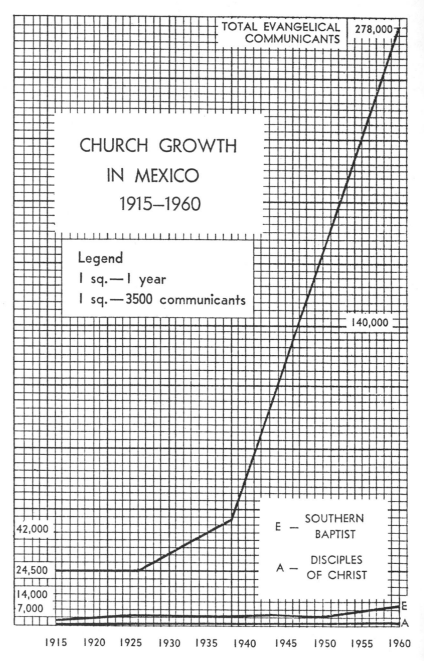

CHURCH GROWTH
IN MEXICO
1915–1960

Legend
1 sq.—1 year
1 sq.—3500 communicants

TOTAL EVANGELICAL
COMMUNICANTS

278,000

140,000

42,000

24,500

14,000
7,000

E — SOUTHERN
BAPTIST

A — DISCIPLES
OF CHRIST

1915 1920 1925 1930 1935 1940 1945 1950 1955 1960

(Source: Donald McGavran, John Huegel, and Jack Taylor, *Church Growth in Mexico*. Grand Rapids, Michigan: Wm. B. Eerdmans Publishing Company, 1963. p. 16)

barred from entry. The Inquisition ruled in Mexico for two hundred years and made sure that any who stole their way into Mexico were ferreted out and killed. As the power of the Inquisition weakened, a few Protestants did come in. At first they could not be buried in cemeteries nor could they build churches in which to worship. Later, when Protestant churches were built, they were often burned. The feeling of the ignorant masses and of the classes was one of superstitious and fanatical opposition to any variety of biblical faith. Innumerable instances could be recounted. For example, when the first Evangelical lady in Villahermosa, Tabasco, had a baby, a Roman Catholic woman ran through the streets shouting that the *Protestante* baby had been born with horns and a tail!

The chaos of war and revolution also slowed down the growth of the churches. From 1910 to 1918 armies marched. Passions burned hot. Anti-Americanism, fomented by oil imperialism and punitive expeditions into Mexico, brought about frequent flares of anti-missionary feeling. In 1914 missionaries felt they had to leave the country and could not come back for several years. In its desperate attempts to free itself from the domination of the foreign Roman Catholic hierarchy, the government of Mexico passed laws which seemed to damage Protestant missions. After the agrarian revolution, the anti-clerical and anti-religion parties made it difficult for the Protestants in several provinces, notably Tabasco, where all priests and ministers were barred from the state. Church services were not allowed. Images of saints were ordered buried and Bibles were ordered burned. The drive to free the State from Roman Catholic domination placed all education in the hands of the State and led some missionaries to close their schools. Since others remained open, closure may not have been really necessary.

Only since 1935 has there been that widespread civil peace which allows regular, orderly work. In the disturbed times before 1935, therefore, some Evangelical Churches grew slowly and with many setbacks. Some, however, prospered. Contrasting the two yields some insights into the nature of church growth.

Internal elements also slowed down growth.

The closeness to the United States and the ease with which missionaries could come into Mexico often resulted in two or more Evangelical denominations working in the same towns and cities. Free competition, which has marked the various Branches of the Church of Christ in North America, marked missions in Mexico. Despite nine missions agreeing in 1917 to work according to comity, competition continued. Five large missions stayed out of comity. So did national Churches and later missions from North America, such as the Pentecostals and Churches of God.

It is often asserted that competition slowed down the Evangelical movement; yet it must be granted that the most rapidly growing Churches in Mexico, which are blazing a trail for all Evangelicals and softening up the opposition in innumerable places, would never have had their wide influence if they had allowed the comity system to limit their field.

Indeed, some observers maintain that the Cincinnati Plan, by which the 1917 comity assignments were made, was really detrimental to the Protestant cause. It jolted all missions badly, severing them from some of their churches. It divided Evangelicals into Co-operators and Intruders. It proceeded on the erroneous assumption that one mission board would do all that could possibly be done in a vast population. Had comity been strictly observed, the Congregational Church, with about 300 members in 9 small, static churches (1962 figures), would today be the only Protestant force in 800-mile-long Sinaloa, an increasingly responsive state.

Another internal obstacle to growth was that, faced with high resistance, some missions turned to the "mission station approach." The process was this. When converts, who were few and far between, constantly faced stone, torch and gun from the Roman Catholic Church, Evangelicals were driven to gradualism. They undertook not direct conversion but enterprises "which did something else now so that the Evangelical Church could grow later on." A missionary in the twenties and thirties describing the work of his mission wrote, "We have wonderful opportunities to have warm, personal relationships with the outstanding business and professional people of the city. Our school opens the door for friendship with wonderful people." Gradualism may have been necessary in some cases, but a gradualistic enterprise, once established, has a habit of continuing long after it is unnecessary.

In the same way some missions retreated into service institutions. "If they will not hear the Gospel and obey Christ's call, let us serve them lovingly." "If the government will not let us preach, let us minister quietly in the name of Christ." The dream of influencing the educated classes, already so violently anti-clerical in many parts of Latin America, led to the establishment of schools. . . .

Another internal element which led to non-growing churches was the precarious position of an exposed minority. Protestant standards were high. Ministers and missionaries were preaching that faith in Christ redeems personally and socially. Those who backslid into man or woman trouble, drink, or worldliness, dropped out of the church. They seldom went back to Rome. They were just "lost to the world." Losses also took place to Rome through marriage. Small Evangelical groups have even smaller numbers of adolescent boys and girls. When these get married to Roman Catholics, sometimes the partner becomes an Evangelical; but often the Evangelical becomes a Roman Catholic. Fervent denominations have low losses through marriage. The less fervent have high losses. Other losses take place when young people from the very small Protestant minority move from *ranchos* to the city. They may find and unite with a church, but often they are lost.

Where these three kinds of losses are larger than the gains by evangelism, there the church stagnates. A sealed-off mentality develops. A brave little band of 15 to 50 Christians remains. These Christians hang onto their faith and their church, but they do not do much evangelism. Little churches characterize many towns, *pueblos,* and *ranchos,* especially in some states and denominations. Sometimes these churches die, but more often they struggle on bravely for years.

Where mission institutions are found, there the sealed-off church often grows to a membership of 80, 100, or even 200. The institutions give prestige to the church and education, fellowship, and encouragement to the young Evangelicals. But mission station churches seldom multiply. Their members often are educated men and women and firm Evangelicals. They gain by biological growth (their children grow up as Evangelicals) and by an occasional conversion. They lose when their members move or lapse to the world. Because they want to get along with their neighbors, they hesitate to be aggressively evangelistic. Some have paid a high price for their faith and believe it is well to be careful.

Furthermore, near institutions a curious condition is commonly found which inhibits growth. Members of the institutional staff (nationals and missionaries) come to know each other extremely well. Their conversation is inevitably about mutual interests, problems, equipment, undertakings, friends, students, patients, and employees. This is their world. Staff members always go to church and often comprise its leadership. Observe them coming out of church, and you will see them and hear them moving inside their own world. A potential convert approaches any church timidly, sits on the back seats, hesitates to find or sing unfamiliar hymns, and follows the service with difficulty. After church he hurries out and away as fast as he can. Often he goes away without anyone speaking to him. But even if active Christians make it a point to speak to him and introduce him to several, there is little to talk about because he is not of their world. This is especially the case if he is a country man.

The more Christian the church, the more love it manifests among the members, the more they are truly one family, the more difficult it is for newcomers to become a real part of its specialized world. Indeed, the only way old Christians (missionaries and members) of a friendly institutional church can become evangelistically potent is to give enough time and prayer to personal evangelism so that considerable numbers of outside persons become a part of their world. About these persons they converse—and pray—frequently. When such persons come to church, the old Christians welcome them, sit with them, make them feel at home in the service, and after worship talk easily to *them* rather than to old friends!

Another element causing some churches to be static is their national leadership. One frequently hears it said that a cure for a static church is to turn it over to the nationals, but this is not necessarily true. Whether the leaders' mother tongue is English or Spanish, they all face the same conditions, the same encirclement, the same impenetrable barrier of a friendly family. Just as one generation of missionaries can transmit low expectations and gradualistic techniques to their successor missionaries, so can they to their successor nationals. In general, if a Church was growing before control passed to nationals, it will continue growing under them. If it was not growing, it will continue static. Both nationals and missionaries, therefore, should learn all they can about church growth and practice all they learn.

Another potent element making for little growth in Mexico is the Shadow of the North. Denominations in the United States, facing the situation there, develop a way of life which enables their congregations to survive and grow. This way is unconsciously followed by their church members and is taught in their seminaries. Missionaries then come to Mexico with the "denominational ways of doing things," which we call "cultural overhangs." Some overhangs are highly detrimental to the multiplication of churches in Mexico. . . .

A final internal factor which inhibits church growth is a low view of the Church, a view where open confession of Christ followed by responsible membership in His Church is not that for which we should immediately labor. The low view of the Church adopts things other than church membership as the primary goal of mission.

In Mexico a low view develops easily. A typical process is described below. For three hundred years the Roman Catholic Church implanted in all Mexicans an intense repugnance to the thought of "becoming Protestants." The Inquisition burned "heretics, sorcerers, bigamists, and protestants." The very word "Protestant" was despised. Till late in the nineteenth century, the establishment of an Evangelical Church by Mexicans was not only impossible, but the thought itself would have been rejected as vile.

Under these circumstances, missionaries of the true, apostolic, catholic and biblical faith found that a chief way to open the closed citadel of the people's mind was to place in men's hands a copy of the Bible. . . .

To get people to "read the Bible" was so desirable an end that it sometimes eclipsed the supreme need for their becoming responsible members of the Church of Christ and establishing churches.[4]

—Donald McGavran
Church Growth in Mexico

* * * * *

1. To what extent and under what circumstances do external factors retard church growth? Do they always function as a negative force?

2. What effects would comity have on church growth? Give strengths and weaknesses of the comity system from the church growth viewpoint.

3. McGavran states: "Gradualism may have been necessary in some cases. . . ." What circumstances, in your opinion, constitute such cases?

4. The arrested growth is caused by either lack of accession or membership leakage or both. What are some of the causes of membership leakage (ways out of the church)?

5. Define in your own words "cultural overhang." What examples can you give to illustrate the concept?

29: OBSTRUCTIONS TO GROWTH IN TONGA

The path to conversion has, for many Tonga, frequently been fraught with obstacles or blocked by resistance to change. Sometimes the people have misinterpreted the primary purpose of the missionaries and instead of being viewed as a herald of a more excellent Way, the missionary has often been looked upon as a crusader against drunkenness and polygyny. The animist has seen little evidence of any congeniality between the new way and his old pattern of existence, nor can he detect anything that is distinctly better than what he already possesses.

We do not minimize the transformation which must take place in the life of every individual who wishes to accept, obey, and surrender to Christ Jesus as Lord, but in seeking to prepare the way for such a drastic change, it is our responsibility to remove every barrier that we possibly can from the path of the hearer *except the cross of Christ.*

At the cross the believer makes his decision to die with Christ, and to appropriate the blood of Christ to blot out his sins. There each person publicly confesses and demonstrates his allegiance to the King of Kings, and only then does the convert have the power to overcome the sin in his life. The Spirit of God will then be able to bear fruit in his life and perfect him.

Requiring a man to stop getting drunk, to put away all but one of his wives, or to desist from worshipping "evil spirits" *before* he becomes a Christian, is like asking a man to lift himself out of the mire by his own bootstraps. It is impossible for a man to demonstrate the fruits of the Spirit without the Spirit.

I believe that throughout Tongaland there are four major obstructions to church growth. They are: (1) the problem of widespread drunkenness, (2) polygyny, (3) the equation of "church" and "school" by many of the people, and (4) the slow growth resulting from over-institutionalized mission.

DRUNKENNESS

Almost invariably the problem of drunkenness has been mentioned at the top of the list by Tonga church leaders as the main reason for reversion and unfaithfulness in church attendance. It has also proved an obstruction to those who might otherwise become Christians. . . .

I personally find it extremely difficult to determine the extent to which beer-drinking is involved in Tonga religious rites and rituals, but I believe beer-drinking is losing its religious connections and is now being engaged in more out of sheer pleasure than anything else. To the women it is a source of income and independence, but to men the beer party means association, story-telling and a place to pass the day. . . .

In order to get to the root of the problem of drinking, we must try to uncover as many of the reasons for this practice as possible. . . .

There are, in my opinion, at least five reasons for beer-drinking and drunkenness in Tonga society:

1. It has religious significance in the performance of certain rites, rituals, and sacrifices.
2. It is one attempt to achieve and maintain status.
3. It is a display of wealth.
4. It is an attempt to overcome the anxieties and strains of a people whose culture is undergoing change and upheaval.
5. The village beer party is an occasion for association.

Obviously, through beer-drinking and drunkenness *these people are trying to satisfy felt needs.* They are desirous of human dignity and purpose, and of peace with the supernatural. They want others to like them and crave fellowship and association. They long for security and peace of mind in the face of a rapidly changing environment. This many-faceted problem cannot be resolved by castigation and negative preaching.

I sincerely believe that Christ through His Body can provide an answer to every one of these needs. They can be satisfied within the Church. People must be led to see that Christianity *is more than just "no beer-drinking."* By sensing the needs of the Tonga heart we can lead him into a new relationship with Christ, and his deepest desires will be fulfilled within the fellowship of the saints.

Perhaps non-alcoholic substitutes could be found to take the place of intoxicating drink. *Mukande* (sweet beer) might fill the void left by the removal of *bukoko* (alcoholic beer).

It might also be better for the Church, while warring earnestly against drunkenness and outlawing religious drinking, to cease insisting on the non-biblical prerequisite for baptism: that penitent sinners renounce beer-drinking.

THE CHRISTIAN ATTITUDE TOWARD POLYGYNY

For decades there has been a basic conflict between Christianity and African traditional life on the subject of polygyny. Frequently the fact that a man has been involved in a longstanding polygynous union becomes a seemingly insurmountable barrier to his becoming a Christian. Missionaries cannot agree upon what course they should follow.

I think that it is about time that Western missionaries take a hard second look at this problem regarding which we know so little and upon which the New Testament is silent. . . .

Generally speaking, one of three positions has been most favored by Missions in Africa regarding polygynists: (1) some refuse to baptize husbands, wives, or children in a polygynous household; (2) others would baptize the wives and children but refuse the husband, and (3) a very few permit the baptism of the polygynous husband and his family in the first generation only. I firmly believe that we should accept the third position.

By accepting the man in the state in which he has been called (1 Corinthians 7:17-24) we do not indiscriminately destroy his household, create fatherless children, drive his divorced wives into adultery or prostitution, or alienate forever the lineage of his divorced wives.

> For further discussion of polygyny, refer to Unit 13.

If we adopt the second view, however, Christianity becomes (in the minds of pagan people) an ideology to be resisted at all costs for it destroys households and tears apart the tribal solidarity. Two more heinous crimes could hardly be found in African traditional society. Many will be unable to see the blessed Christ because His servants have placed an unnecessary barrier before the polygynous pagan. . . .

There can be no doubt concerning the New Testament ideal for Christian monogamy. In the Bible marriage is depicted as a spiritual-moral tie between man and wife; two who become one flesh (Mark 10:6-9). The sexual relationship is an essential element, but certainly not the all-determining factor. Marriage in the Bible also reflects the closeness of the spiritual relationship between Christ and His Church (Ephesians 5:29-33).

This high view of the worth of woman in Christianity does not exist in traditional Tonga society. The basic evil in pagan marriage is *the low view of woman*. It is not confined to polygynous unions, but also exists in monogamous marriages.

I believe that we should teach the obvious monogamic ideal of the New Testament to those who have obeyed Christ as their Savior and who have become members of His Church, but that such teaching should be a part of our *post-baptismal instruction, not our pre-baptismal requirements*. . . .

EQUATING CHURCH AND SCHOOL

There is almost no distinction between "church" and "school" in the minds of many Africans. Christianity has become a classroom religion in Africa, a misconception which is largely responsible for the disproportionate ratio of school children to adult members in local congregations throughout Africa.

A common response by adult men when invited to church is, "I cannot go to school with children. Church is only for children and women." He is saying that he is *above* what he conceives the Church to be. It would be an affront to his social position to require him to learn along with the children of his village. As long as he continues to conceptualize the Church in such terms, this equation of church and school will remain an obstruction to church growth. This is a problem of meaning to which solutions must be found as soon as possible. It is particularly acute in those areas where the school emphasis has been the strongest.

History shows that often the first thing that missionaries brought to a community was a school. After it was established and operating as efficiently as could be expected under the circumstances, a few children would usually be converted by the Christian teacher, and perhaps an adult or two would also accept Christ. But the place where they met was always in the school building, where there were enough chairs for everyone and the little congregation could find shelter from rain and cold.

In many of the Sunday services the schoolteacher is the monolithic director of all of the worship activities. He leads the singing, presides at the communion, preaches the sermon and teaches the Sunday school lessons. Sunday services are built around him; he is in charge of the hymnals, Bibles, and the order of worship. So much depends upon him that when he vacillates the whole congregation wavers. When school closes for vacation, church services are discontinued until school resumes.

As we have already noted, the Churches of Christ turned over their village schools to the government in 1965. Shortly after this handover, many of the village "school churches" were defunct and so-called "Christian" teachers no longer felt any responsibility for the church. Some even forbade the congregation to meet in their school buildings for services. As the teacher went, so the church went, in so many cases. At least ten churches died overnight. . . .

The basic misinterpretation of the relationship between the church and the school still exists in many villages where schools have been operated by the church at one time or another and it may be years before the church assumes the preeminent position in the village. I do not know the answer to this dilemma, but perhaps what one Christian schoolteacher has done may be a partial solution to the problem. He has concentrated on planting a church in a nearby village where they do not have a school, and he is encouraging the church members to erect their own church building and meet in their own village.

Another way to overcome this obstruction to church expansion is to begin preaching Christ and persuading *winnable units* to accept Him at one time. This will involve starting with adults instead of children. They will begin to see that God has a message for *them* and that *they* are in a position to make the decision to accept or reject.

The school church has an extremely limited power of penetration within its village environment, and unless a concentrated effort is made to convert the pagan power structure and the winnable adults within the village, congregations with this school-church complex will continue to be dependent upon the Christian teacher or upon visits by missionaries to keep them infused with life.

INSTITUTIONALISM AND MISSION-STATION CENTEREDNESS

Introversion, isolation, and a centralized sedentary organization usually characterize *institutionalism*. This inward-looking kind of mission work is better known in mission theory as *mission-station centeredness*. The Church is faced with this obstruction in Tongaland, and if it is to minister Christ to 270,000 Tongas, it must grapple with this obstacle to church growth, and then find and implement radical new methods by which it can break out of this deadening centralization.

Mission-station centeredness closely resembles the church-building centeredness which afflicts most American churches. Instead of the building or mission station serving as a base for outreach into its immediate area, it becomes a place where its members or missionaries find security, speak the same theological language, enjoy one another's association, and from which they make periodic appeals to the world to come and learn of Jesus Christ. As introversion increases, contact with the totally lost decreases. Conversation and fellowship among the saved takes precedence over witnessing to the lost.

The longer this church continues its inward emphasis or extends its period of consolidation, the greater is the tendency for it to begin erecting a bigger, more comfortable building, padding its pews, installing softer and thicker carpets, organizing itself into committees and planning programs, and losing sight of the pressing human needs of salvation and compassion which abound on its doorstep and around the world. The church which has turned its eyes toward itself becomes sedentary, selfish, and isolated. It becomes an institution, not the living body of Christ.

Similarly, when a mission station becomes self-centered and introverted it begins to concentrate upon the erection of bigger and better buildings, its missionaries find association among themselves instead of with the nationals and devote practically all of their time to administrative pursuits, negotiations with contractors and management of building, and teaching and healing projects. Like the home church, the sensitivity of its missionary personnel to human needs and to the thousands of precious people for whom Christ died who live within its area of influence is lost in the hustle and bustle of an isolated and introverted institution. . . .

Having lived or worked for a total of twenty years on various mission stations among the Tonga, there are several reasons why I believe that institutionalism and mission-station centeredness almost always obstruct rather than propagate the Church of Jesus Christ.

The institution tends to become an end in itself. Instead of the school, hospital, or Bible school being the fruit of (and the responsibility of) the national churches, the institution becomes the tree which supports the churches. The institution, in this case, grows out of the desires of the missionaries for the people, rather than out of needs which the national churches recognize and for which they assume most of the responsibility

. . . An institution which has become the end in itself has an insatiable appetite for missionary personnel and resources.

Institutions take priority over evangelism in the deployment of missionary personnel. By their very nature mission institutions demand routine, consistency, and continuity. Schools do not open and close their doors at random. Schedules have to be made and met. There have to be enough teachers and sufficient funds to enable a school to function. When the need for an additional worker in an institution arises, usually a missionary is either persuaded to offer his assistance "on a temporary basis" or he is transferred from evangelistic work to the institution. The institution comes first, it must go on, evangelism and post-baptismal indoctrination can wait. . . .

Institutions receive financial priority over evangelistic and church-planting budgets. It is often argued that the institution must be perpetuated because so much time, energy, and money have already been invested in it . . . When institutions receive top priority in terms of missionary personnel and money, it is extremely difficult, if not impossible, to convince people that Christ and His Church are more important than our nice-looking school. Not only do we, as missionaries, forget our main goal, but what is more tragic, the nationals see external manifestations which do not correspond with our inward intentions. This severely impedes church growth.

Institutions fail to produce church growth proportionate to the financial investments in them. . . .

In 1968, over 90 percent of the money contributed by American Churches of Christ and individuals for their missions in Tongaland was expended on the secondary school at Namwianga. Of course, one might point out that 1968 was a year of construction and that the costs were unusually high. But, unless the proportion changes drastically in the future, this one institution alone will continue to consume by far the largest slice of the financial pie.

I believe that a number of questions need to be raised concerning this tremendous expenditure in terms of personnel and money and the overall effectiveness of such an institutional approach:

1. Are the teen-aged graduates of this Christian secondary school *actually* becoming the leaders of the churches?
2. Are they planting churches or forming the nuclei of churches where they work or live after graduation?
3. Are we training the children of Christian parents who want a Christian education for their children or are we using the school as an evangelistic tool?
4. Is the institution maintaining a high level of spirituality and evangelistic fervor?
5. Is it helping to build strong churches?
6. Is it possible, within five years, for national churches to assume its support and operation in view of the nationalization of education by the Zambian government?

7. Provided the Zambian government permits a church-supported educational institution to exist, would national Christians be willing and financially capable of taking over the school within five years?
8. Do the national Christians consider the school theirs, or do they view it as a foreign imposition?

If these questions cannot be answered in the affirmative, it would be my conviction that this Mission should take a long, hard look at what its real goals are. . . .

Institutionalism may have harmful effects upon missionary personnel. Living and working within an isolated community such as an introverted mission station or institution can contribute to spiritual stagnation. This does not happen to everyone, but in talking intimately with many missionaries and having had some years of personal experience, the following harmful attitudes may develop:

1. Routine and the environment of slow growth in the institution rob missionaries of their sense of urgency to proclaim the Gospel.
2. Inward-looking mission stations insulate missionaries from the actual line of conflict where souls can and are being won to Christ.
3. Isolation from village nationals often fosters racial superiority.
4. Local loyalties to a particular institution increase the missionary's desire to maintain control.
5. Language study is thwarted because missionaries usually have contact only with English-speaking students and staff on the mission station.
6. Routine and pressing duties of the mission station often crowd out time for God, and the spiritual life of the missionary suffers.
7. Missionaries become conditioned to slow growth and consequently are not sensitive to areas of receptivity.

Institutionalism may have harmful effects upon national Christians. It became apparent to me during the 1968 church growth survey that mission-station centeredness had adversely affected the attitudes of village Christians toward Christ and toward the Mission.

1. They failed to see that Christ was the real purpose for the existence of the institution.
2. Church planting was relegated to a role secondary to the operation of efficient mission institutions.
3. Village Christians resented the neglect by missionaries who claimed they had the Words of Life but who were too involved in duties at the mission station.[5]

—Stan Shewmaker
Tonga Christianity

* * * * *

1. Beer-drinking in Tonga society is said to satisfy felt needs of the people. What are these needs? Discuss the ways in which the church as the body of Christ can provide answers to these needs. What do you think are the felt needs of the people in America today? How can the church meet these needs?

2. What are the church growth implications to each of the three positions taken by the Christian mission in Africa toward polygyny? Which position do you favor? Why?

3. The school approach in Africa seems to be an effective method of evangelism for children. But what are the weaknesses of this approach?

4. What is the function of a mission institution in its relationship to the local church and to church growth? What is the function of a church-related school in America?

5. Note the elements in the Tonga mission which lead to mission introversion. How can a mission protect itself from becoming isolationistic? Is it possible that some American churches may likewise suffer from introversion? What can American churches do to insure that they will remain the church and not become simply an institution to be perpetuated at all costs?

PART IV

PLANNING FOR CHURCH GROWTH

Church growth thinking not only affects the missionary's work on the mission field, but it also alters the sending church's method of relating to the emerging national churches. In addition, it revises the traditional position of the missionary in relation to both the mission and the sending church. The local congregation, moreover, faces added responsibilities in selecting, sending, and sustaining missionaries who will meet church growth standards. The seventh chapter will look at these relationships from the church growth point of view, suggesting certain church growth standards and raising questions in areas where additional thinking is needed, such as the always difficult problem which arises when an emerging national church believes itself ready for autonomy.

The eighth chapter introduces the perennial problem in mission outreach: money. If church growth theorists are right, then the American dollar can do as much harm as good for the cause of Christ, if it creates a dependency upon foreign support and retards independence and growth. Therefore, every contribution to mission must be given according to principles of wise stewardship, keeping in mind the church growth emphases discussed in chapter 2. Where should the dollar go—and why? Planning for church growth demands fiscal responsibility. Chapter 8 provides guidelines for responsible financial planning.

Chapter 7
MISSION-CHURCH RELATIONSHIPS

In the pioneering days of modern missions, the great adventurers for Christ braved the perils of primitive conditions to rescue individuals from the everlasting fires. The necessity of personal salvation was rightly emphasized, but the teaching that a Christian is a member of the body of Christ, the church, was frequently neglected. In the twentieth century this imbalance has been corrected, thanks, interestingly enough, largely to the effort of missions.

> Missionary emphasis today is upon the church ... We are concerned with the mission of the church, conceived of as a world-wide fellowship charged with the responsibility for the evangelization of the world. The modern "rediscovery of the church," of which we read and hear so much, was, in fact, largely a missionary achievement. It arose with the discovery on the mission field of the church as fellowship, as *koinonia*. Within thousands of small groups of believers scattered throughout the world, the miracle of first century Christian fellowship has been re-enacted before our eyes. Men and women, after experiencing the transformed life "in Christ" or "in the Spirit," have found themselves bound with an incredible new bond to others sharing the same life, in a fellowship transcending former barriers of class or caste or race.[1]

When a person is received by Christ, he is accepted into the community of believers who are also joined to Him. The believer is not only one with Christ but he is also one with fellow Christians.

The church growth movement stands with the ecumenical movement in this emphasis upon the church. It is unique, however, in its persistent question concerning every missionary activity: "Does it assist the growth of the church?" All kinds of missionary endeavors are good, but the primary task is always church planting. Therefore, church growth theorists can readily assent to Professor Bavinck's carefully constructed definition of missions because of its union of the individual believer's response to the invitation of Christ and his involvement as a member of Christ's body, the church:

> Missions is that activity of the church—in essence it is nothing else than an activity of Christ, exercised through the church—through

which the church, in this interim period, in which the end is post-poned, calls the peoples of the earth to repentance and to faith in Christ, so that they may be made his disciples and through baptism be incorporated into the fellowship of those who await the coming of the kingdom.[2]

What happens, then, to the newly incorporated disciples when their new church matures sufficiently to achieve independence of the mission and the sending church? In order to suggest some answers to this question, this chapter will introduce the concept "indigenous church" and present some of the tensions which arise when the new church identifies itself as something other than the mission. In addition, the chapter will suggest the continuing role of the sending church in today's mission endeavor.

30: THE INDIGENOUS CHURCH

The greatest nineteenth-century mission theorist, Henry Venn, contributed to missionary thinking the term *indigenous church*. In a paper entitled "Native Church Organization," published by the Church Missionary Society, Venn outlined the purpose of the society to be

> the development of Native Churches, with a view to their ultimate settlement upon a self-supporting, self-governing and self-extending system. When this settlement has been effected, the Mission will have attained its euthanasia, and the missionary and all missionary agency can be transferred to the regions beyond.[3]

For decades Venn was a voice in the wilderness, his emphasis upon indigeneity being consistently ignored by denominational leaders and missionaries alike. The result was a growing dependence of the new converts upon missionaries and missions. The reasons for this paternalism are manifold: a conscious or sub-conscious sense of personal or cultural superiority on the part of the missionary or sending agency; a need to dominate; a need to be considered indispensable; a hesitancy to trust the Holy Spirit to guide the new converts into the truth; a reliance upon money—usually foreign —to solve the social problems of the underdeveloped country; a confusion of the essence of the gospel with the cultural accretions of the "civilized" sending countries. This list could obviously be expanded.

Church growth theorists resist this dependence upon foreign leadership and finances for a most pragmatic reason: indigenous churches grow; dependent congregations do not. While not at all opposed to the use of foreign leadership and money to assist churches grow, church growth theory resists long-term investments of either, having accumulated evidence that large dependent institutions (like hospitals or schools) and congregations relying upon foreign dollars to pay for pastors simply do not become evangelistic centers. Reliance upon foreign provisions leads to adoption of foreign worship and cultural practices—and further alienation from native customs and people.

> The particularity of a church is what distinguishes it from every other church. The words *indigenous* and *church* are in tension. One represents something particular and unreproducible, and the other points to what is everywhere the same. No general type of thing called an "indigenous church" exists; there are only concrete indigenous churches. Every Christian community—if it is the church at all—represents an accommodation of the universal, God-given basis to a particular human setting.[4]
>
> —James A. Scherer
> *Missionary, Go Home!*

167

Let me describe briefly two congregations with whom I have worshipped myself. They have much in common, being both Melanesian with all the cultural similarities which belong to the Melanesian people in general. They both have had a sufficiently long period of Christian history to have developed their character as third generation congregations. They were evangelized by missionaries of the same denomination, from the same country, with the same theological background, training and methods of support. We might expect these congregations to be very similar, yet this is not so.

One congregation was worshipping with a great deal of congregational participation, the male and female roles being widely distributed, the music had a distinctly Melanesian quality about it and was unaccompanied, the choir-master was one of the people, and so was the preacher, (although occasionally a missionary preached, always in the native language), the offering was received after an indigenous pattern, from time to time individuals in the congregation expressed appreciation of some point with a traditional exclamation. The people were clearly at worship and enjoying themselves.

The other congregation was served by a missionary. It was a monolithic service. He led everything, announced everything, said everything. The choir was as good as in the other congregation, but was led by a foreigner (a Melanesian from another area), the music was foreign, the collection was received in a plate passed round in the western way, the sermon was often in English, and when not so it was frequently translated, the congregation sat and listened and did not participate in any other way. What groups they had and Sunday School classes were run by foreigners in civil positions in the area. The former congregation had both a mission and service outreach, the latter had a few small projects organized and run by the missionary and his wife. This is just the precise difference between an indigenous and a foreign Church. I know them both personally and I repeat that they have sprung from the same sending community and denomination.[5]

—A. R. Tippett
Verdict Theology in Missionary Theory

Appreciation for the indigenous church has grown recently in ecumenical, evangelical, and church growth circles. Missiologists have offered several statements concerning the genius of the church in adapting its universal character to local settings. Such statements presuppose clear delineation of the essential nature of the church and non-essential cultural practice. They separate what must identify the church in every locality and must be maintained in order for the church to be the church from those practices that are helpful adaptations to the customs of a people. With this distinction in mind, the Willingen report, "The Indigenous Church—the Universal Church in Its Local Setting," describes the marks of indigeneity. Scherer summarizes them as follows:

> Willingen stressed four in particular: (1) relatedness to the soil —ability to make elements of local cultures captive to Christ so that the Christian message may become an integral part of the life and experience of a people; (2) possession of an adequately trained ministry and the willingness to adapt the pattern of the ministry to local requirements; (3) an inner spiritual life issuing in responsibility for the nurture of the Christian community and missionary witness to the evangelized; and (4) membership in the church universal, expressed in supraracial, supranational witness, with a sense of partnership in obedience and mutual help toward other churches of the ecumenical fellowship.[6]

* * * * *

1. Scherer says "No general type of thing called an 'indigenous church' exists; there are only concrete indigenous churches." What does he mean?

2. Which is more important—to foster indigenous churches or growing churches? Or can the two be separated?

3. What are some of the indigenous characteristics of the American church you attend?

4. The unit closes with the Willingen statement. This is not a policy written by church growth thinkers. Would a church growth leader have given any different emphasis to the statement?

The new appreciation for the independent national church which has grown in recent decades has introduced tensions into mission-church relations. The movement from paternalism to fraternalism, with mission and infant church co-existing in many lands, has resulted in uneasy relations in several places. Recently the cry from national churches for either merger of the two or absorption of the mission into the church has grown insistent. Missionary personnel and funds have increasingly been turned over to the control of the younger churches, with debatable results.

Alfred Larson discusses four kinds of mission-church relationships which can exist on a mission field. His objective treatment of the subject does not support any one to the exclusion of the other three, but does stress the primacy of church growth and raises questions which must be answered on every mission field.

Following Larson's study is Louis L. King's reminder that "no mission-church relationship pattern is fully ideal."

* * * * *

CHURCH-MISSION RELATIONSHIP—A FUSED PARTNERSHIP

In the Bible we have a sovereign declaration, "I will build my church; and the gates of hell shall not prevail against it" (Matthew 16:18). No specific location was indicated by the Lord Jesus, nor were any qualifying limitations placed on this statement.

This emphasis on the church was predominant in the writings of the New Testament.

As interdenominational mission organizations, we ask ourselves: What is the most effective and God-honoring way to relate our programs to the national churches which have been brought into being through our ministries?

In our strategy for the years before us, we recognize that the national church is in the forefront, not the mission. It is the church, not the mission, which is the abiding body and which must dominate in the church-mission relationship.

There are a number of questions before us: Acknowledging that the mission societies are accidents of history rather than Biblical ideals, what is the place today of the interdenominational mission society? When is a national church truly autonomous? Is there a particular pattern of church-mission relationship which would serve as an ideal for all fields of the world? Is the program of church-mission cooperation conditioned by cultural, political, psychological and other factors?

The interdenominational mission relates to the sending church, in a sense, as a service agency while maintaining a separate administration and organizational structure. Generally speaking, this relationship to the sending church has been acceptable, whereas the relationship to the receiving church has become increasingly more complex through the years.

In an article on mission-church relationships, Dr. Peters indicates that there are being advocated these four patterns of relationship with the receiving church:

1. The pattern of complete organizational disassociation of mission and church.
2. The pattern of fraternal partnership and obedience.
3. The pattern of mission partnership and missionary servantship.
4. The pattern of partnership of equality and mutuality.[7]

Let us define briefly these patterns of mission-church relationship:

1. The pattern of complete organizational disassociation of mission and church: Here the mission and church are two autonomous bodies with separate administrations cooperating together. The mission carries the responsibility of evangelizing and establishing churches, and these churches become a part of the national church organization. The missionary, then, does not come under the jurisdiction of the national church; rather, the church and mission programs are set up in cooperation one with the other.

2. The second pattern of fraternal partnership and obedience is similar to the preceding one. Both groups remain distinctive and autonomous entities with each group having its own organization, personnel, budget, and program. However, the difference in this pattern is that here the mission functions more or less as a service agency to the national church, loaning workers to the churches for specific projects and also promoting certain projects for the benefit of the church, such as educational institutions, etc.

3. The third pattern is often referred to as Fusion. The Rev. Jean B. Bokeleale, General Secretary of the Churches of Christ in Congo, is a strong advocate of fusion of church and mission. A summary of his presentation of fusion follows:[8]

   a. Disappearance of legal status of the mission in favor of the church.
   b. A missionary becomes a full member of the church and is available to serve in any office of the church.
   c. All equipment and properties come under the ownership of the church, the missionary having priority in certain areas such as a missionary residence.
   d. All finances controlled by the church.
   e. Direct relations, without an intermediary, between the home board of the mission organization and the young church.

In this program of fusion, as advocated by Mr. Bokeleale, the national church becomes responsible for total administration on the field of both church and mission. Therefore, the missionary program as well as the missionaries are integrated into the national structure. Ownership of property, placement of personnel, and all finances come under the administration of the national church.

The missionary in this type of program is usually referred to as a fraternal worker who is assigned to his ministry by the national church and is responsible to the national church. Usually he would still receive his support from home churches through the mission organization, to the national church, and then to him. Dr. Peters, in referring to this pattern, states: "While the mission considers itself a partner of the national church, the missionary becomes a servant of the national church. The missionary partnership has been converted into servantship."[9]

4. The pattern of partnership of equality and mutuality: Dr. Peters writes on this relationship: "Missions must be related to the churches and must become an integral part of the churches, fully involving the national churches. The missionary's ministry must be rendered through the church, but not mainly to the church. Principally, he works neither in the church nor for the church, but with the church. His service is mainly to the unevangelized world. Whatever his official membership may be, he is a full-fledged member of the board of missions and the national church with rights, privileges, and responsibilities, serving in the missionary expansion of the church. This assignment is his by divine calling and mutual agreement between him and his mission and the national church, and cannot be altered by unilateral action either by the mission or the church. Only in this manner is true partnership possible and equality and mutuality evident."[10]

In seeking to establish the recommended pattern for church-mission relationships, certain factors must be kept in mind. Much is said these years on the theme, "From Missions to Mission." The emphasis seems to be that all the church is and does is mission. One could ask the question: If then everything is mission, is anything mission? It seems to be easy to speak of total mission and lose the thrust of missions. It is the concern of missions to press forward, reaching out to the unevangelized. It is our desire and hope to see churches established and growing. Therefore, of necessity, we are deeply involved in training programs in order to establish the younger churches in the Word. In light of our calling to missions, do we continue to be chiefly engaged in outreach to unsaved people or are we becoming largely institutional-minded and more absorbed with the church than the world? Are an increasing portion of our energies being directed to the maintenance of churches and institutions for Christians, when the cutting edge of the church should be reaching out to new frontiers with the Gospel? Has this institutional-mindedness contributed to our lack of mobility and the building of what is termed as the mission-station mind?[11]

In considering the church-mission pattern, we must also give real thought to the question of mutual confidence and trust. As interdenominational mission boards, we draw our support from across the spectrum of Protestant churches in our home countries; yet we invariably form a fellowship of churches in the countries in which we serve. It is our earnest desire to see a burden for missions in these young churches and the pattern of church-

mission relationships ought to be one which will encourage the church to
send out its own missionaries to other areas.[12]

—Alfred Larson
from *Missions in Creative Tension*

* * * * *

NO MISSION-CHURCH RELATIONSHIP PATTERN FULLY IDEAL

Although it is necessary and profitable to learn all that we can about
mission-church relationship, it should not so absorb our attention that the
evangelistic and missionary obligation of the Church is obscured. Further,
the complexities of the subject strongly suggest that our presenting a con-
census opinion about which is the best is ill-advised. There are simply too
many variables to deal with. Whether the church is newly started; large or
small, burdened with institutional responsibilities or unencumbered;
evangelistic and missionary or static—all these factors have to be considered. Also the form of ecclesiastical government and whether the mission is a faith society or a denominational board will make a difference.
And some things discovered to be helpful or hurtful in one country or area
may not be so in another. Differences in cultures, national feelings, and the
selfhood of the church must be taken under advisement.[13]

—Louis L. King
from *Missions in Creative Tension*

* * * * *

GUIDELINES FOR MISSION-CHURCH RELATIONS OVERSEAS

The following, though, should remain constant in any structure of
mission-church relationship:

- The national church rejects the status of dependence and recognizes its own responsibilities. It maintains its independence from
  outside direction or interference. An atmosphere in the mission-
  church relationship is created wherein evangelism and church
  planting are mutually desired and undertaken. The church assumes
  its full stature in Christ, having its own missionary outreach.

- The sending church is permitted to remain missionary in obedience
  to the essential obligation of a true New Testament church. The
  missionary can fulfill his personal, unique, and divine calling as a
  missionary.

- There is frank recognition that the great job which remains to be
  done cannot be accomplished by either the mission or the national
  church working alone but only by the combined operations of both
  working together to fulfill the Great Commission.

• The mission's relationship with the church is primarily at that point in which the church is engaged in witness and mission to the non-Christian world outside its door.[14]

—Louis L. King
from Missions in Creative Tension

★ ★ ★ ★ ★

For Additional Reading in Mission-Church Tensions:

Crossroads in Missions, a William Carey Multibook containing five key books:

Blauw, *The Missionary Nature of the Church* (Lutterworth)

Scherer, *Missionary, Go Home!* (Prentice-Hall)

Beyerhaus and Lefever, *The Responsible Church and Foreign Mission* (Eerdmans)

Street, *On the Growing Edge of the Church* (John Knox Press)

Beaver, *The Missionary between the Times* (Doubleday)

The Future of the Christian World Mission: Studies in Honor of R. Pierce Beaver. Ed. William J. Danker and Wi Jo Kang. Grand Rapids, Michigan: William B. Eerdmans Publishing Company, 1971.

Missions in Crisis, Eric S. Fife and Arthur F. Glasser. Chicago: Inter-Varsity Press, 1961.

Eye of the Storm, Donald McGavran (ed.). Waco, Texas: Word Books Publisher, 1972.

Understanding Church Growth, Donald McGavran. Grand Rapids, Michigan: William B. Eerdmans Publishing Company, 1970.

This unit assumes that whatever the denominational structure, the local congregation plays the key role in the church's mission program. It is in the local church that money is given, prayers are offered, missionaries are recruited. Although a missionary may be commissioned by a denominational board, he still feels "sent" by his home church or another congregation with which he has closely identified. Furthermore, the missionary needs local church identification and fellowship to sustain him abroad. Conversely, the local church needs the missionary to keep its vision focused upon the "fields white unto harvest."

This sense of fellowship between the missionary and the local congregation has become increasingly important in this century for two reasons: the first is a return to apostolic precedent in which local congregations commission the "missionaries," and the second is a reaction to the extreme limits to which the separation between church and mission was carried by some churches, especially in Germany, Holland, and Switzerland:

In most cases the missionary had been trained in a special institution, where the studies were not on the same level of academic excellence as in the universities and the examinations of which were not recognized by the Church. He was then ordained not by the Church but by the missionary society, to the office not of minister of

MISSIONARY RELATIONSHIPS

The missionary has four relationships to maintain in his apostolic ministry: to God, to the people of the land where he is sent, to the newly emerging or already established church in that land, and to his home church which sends him. To each of these he is servant or minister. We have seen something of contemporary problems and issues involved in the second and third. The most fuzzy and uncertain of the relationships is that of the missionary to his home church. One wonders why missionaries do not feel more frustration about this than about any of the others.[15]

* * *

Although the missionary's contact with his sending church is mostly with the mission board, that board of world missions is not the church, but only an agency of it. The missionary should relate directly to the denominational church in its local congregations. The church at every level is the body of the disciples, not the hierarchy or officialdom. The missionary is the servant of the home church not only because he is sent by it to minister the love of Christ

the word and sacraments in the Church but of 'missionary,' a theological concept unknown to the New Testament. When on leave, he could not preach in any

and of the brethren to other people but also because he has an essential ministry within its fellowship.[16]

—R. Pierce Beaver
The Missionary Between the Times

church, since his ordination did not carry with it any right of ministry in his home country. He was simply the employee of a large concern in Europe, submissive to its directions, dependent on it for financial support, responsible to it and to it alone, without direct dependence on or responsibility to any church body.[17]

Such separation from the local church has its obvious limitations. It also denies the New Testament understanding of the church and makes evangelism, which is the task of the whole church, the responsibility of an agency. It denies the local congregation the blessings which come to a church well educated for missionary endeavor:

Missionary training will accomplish for the church what no substitute for it can do. The efficiency of the church will be increased. Indifference, selfishness, parochialism, and spiritual myopia will vanish. The work of every other department of the church will develop when missions flourish. More people will come to the Sunday School and to the church services; more money will flow into the coffers; more spirituality will be seen; more vision will come. The basic vitality of the work will increase, and the blessing of God will rest abundantly on that group of people.[18]

WHAT CAN A LOCAL CONGREGATION DO?

PRAY

Perhaps we ought to say another word about praying for missions. "Prayerful attention" means more than just praying about how much to give. It means more than praying, "God bless the missionaries." It means praying for those who work. It means having such a real concern for it all that our concern will express itself in intercessory prayer.

We don't need to go into the value of intercessory prayer. It is enough to know that missionaries themselves count heavily on it. They know that their work alone can never accomplish its purpose. God must work. They know, too, that God is not reluctant to hear their requests. But they know at the same time that God wants church and missionaries to be united in this task. In prayer they can express some of that spiritual union.[19]

—Harold R. Cook
An Introduction to the Study of Christian Missions

1. How can your congregation be more effectively challenged to pray faithfully for missions?

2. Is it enough to pray for "the work" of the missionaries, or should prayer be directed toward accomplishment of specific goals?

3. For what goals should we pray?

BEWARE THE POWER OF PRAYER

The Moravian example of unbroken intercession twenty-four hours a day leaves no doubt as to the success of such an undertaking. Out of less than every hundred believers one would become a foreign missionary. And to this hour few groups have been able to approach the record set by people whose hearts were aflame with a prayer passion for the lost and dying.[20]
—Harold Lindsell
Missionary Principles and Practice

GIVE

First, spend the Lord's money for missions as carefully as you would for redecorating the church or for a new church organ. Many a church pays less attention to the distributing of its missionary funds than it does to the choice of a new hymnal. The church should know as much about the causes for which its missionary money goes as if each member were investing his personal funds. We should never be less careful of the Lord's money than of our own.

Second, don't give only for the support of individual missionaries or special projects. It is good to have personal contact with individual missionaries, especially if they have come from your church. It is good, also, to have at least a share in their personal support. The same thing is true of special projects, which do have a way of stimulating people to give. But don't stop there.

The reason is this. Who is going to pay the many expenses of carrying on the work? Who will pay for the house the missionary lives in? Who will provide him with the literature and other supplies he needs? Who will pay for his travel, or even for the cost of getting his salary to him at his remote post? Who will pay for the scores of other expenses that are necessary for the carrying on of this mission? Don't forget these needs.

Third, when you do support a missionary, don't feel that your support entitles you to dictate his private life. Support him because you believe he is a faithful representative of the Lord, and do it as unto the Lord. Your stewardship ended when you gave the gift; his began. He is responsible to the Lord, not to you, for using the money wisely. Just as you were responsible to the Lord while it was in your hands.[21]

—Harold Lindsell
Missionary Principles and Practice

For further discussion of the role of money in church growth, see Chapter 8.

EDUCATE

If the leaders of the church can run through a list of this sort and say conscientiously that they are making wise use of a majority of these opportunities, they may feel reasonably satisfied with the work they are doing.

1. An unmistakable missionary spirit running through the Sunday church services.
2. A pronounced missionary emphasis in each congregational organization, particularly the young people's fellowship, the women's association, and the men's brotherhood.
3. Full use of vacation and weekday church schools for the purposes of missionary education.
4. A broad, congregation-wide utilization of any special missionary auxiliaries.
5. A consistent program of missionary education in the Sunday church school.
6. Extensive missionary giving and service activities.
7. Frequent first-hand contacts with missions at home and abroad—the people, the work, the missionaries.
8. Abundant second-hand contacts through audio-visual materials, reading, stories, and dramatization.

9. Proper observance of periods devoted to special missionary emphasis.
10. A continuous program of training leaders in missionary education.[22]

—Nevin C. Harner and David D. Baker.
Missionary Education in Your Church

THE PASTOR AS EDUCATOR

The pastor is a preacher, and the pulpit is his throne. That pulpit should ever reflect his passion and concern for missions. He should preach definite missionary sermons and do so regularly. His sermons not directly related to missions should include allusions to missions and illustrations taken from missionary experience. He should place before his people the needs of the world, the urgency of the task, the opportunities and open doors before their feet, the need for prayer, self-denial and consecration. The sermons themselves should ground the people in the basic principles, giving them the facts of the matter; they should show men what their duty is; they should bring them to the place where they will do something in response to all of the foregoing. Ultimately, all that is done and said is designed to secure results, and the results will demonstrate pragmatically whether what has been said is effective.[23]

—Harold Lindsell
Missionary Principles and Practice

★ ★ ★

No one can possibly take the place of the preacher as a missionary leader. He is the main reliance of his people for spiritual things, and as such he must be informed on the world mission of the Church, or he fails at the very base line of ministerial preparation. This seems little to ask of an ambassador of Christ; yet busy days, nearby interests, sermon-making, and the tendency of over-burdened man to follow the line of least resistance, will give him trends away from careful education on missions, if he is not careful. If the missionary passion is lacking in his soul, the greater his helplessness as he confronts the world with its unmeasured problems and challenge. In fact, every preacher, it is fair to say, sometime or other must face the question as to whether he himself should be serving in mission lands or at home. His grounds for staying here in his ministry, if based on thoughtful decision and certainty, will bring him unfailing conviction on the great world task itself.[24]

—Stephen J. Corey
*The Preacher and
His Missionary Message*

PREPARE AND SELECT CANDIDATES

The following principles and practices should be a part of any well-constructed congregational mission program.

1. Congregations, instead of being passive "customers" of mission appeals by those who want to go to the mission field, should build into their mission programs a process whereby they "search out from among themselves men of good repute" who have adequate qualifications as well as desire to do foreign evangelism.

2. Congregations must take the initiative to see that families being sent to the field have a basic knowledge of other cultures as well as the language of their field.

3. Novice missionaries should have adequate opportunity to be counseled and advised during their first few months on the field by a stable, experienced missionary who can help them to make the transition to the foreign culture.

4. A process should be devised whereby the missionary advises his supporting congregation in concrete terms relative to his activities on the field, and the supporting congregation should develop valid criterion [sic] by which his work and actions may be evaluated.[25]

—Jack Speer

DEVELOP A MISSION STRATEGY

The local church is focal in missionary strategy. What, may we ask, are we aiming to do in missionary efforts? The answer, in most cases, would be, "To win people to Christ." Let it be granted that this is so. What then? Our continuing purpose is that these believers may be united into local congregations of disciples. It is thus they bear witness to their faith, "show forth His death" in the Lord's Supper, edify one another, and continue steadfastly in the apostles' doctrine, fellowship, and prayers. The apostles always assumed and planned that the followers of Jesus would be gathered into churches.

The people involved in some "liberal" missionary efforts have appeared to believe that it is sufficient to spray people with a light tincture of Christian idealism through general educational efforts and hope that a "climate" favorable to Christianity will be created. In one case, a dozen or more "missionaries" served as educators for more than a decade without even one church being established. Finally, after about fifteen years, one church was organized. Surely, the apostle Paul, even in pagan idolatrous cities, did not wait fifteen months, much less fifteen years, before organizing a church.

On the other hand, some "conservative" mission efforts are directed at beaming radio broadcasts and distributing literature over wide areas without, in many cases, making very strenuous efforts to correlate this activity with the establishing of churches. There is "influence" for Christ, there are "words" for Christ, there are inquiries about New Testament Christianity.

Yes, yes! But where are the churches? This must be our insistent, persistent, and, some may say, impertinent, question. But it is absolutely vital, and we must never stop asking it. Where are the churches?

It is good to have orphanages, dispensaries, and hospitals. It is good to have schools and farms and distributors of Bibles. But these are of no permanent value apart from churches. Individuals won to Christ will wither and die in isolation unless they can be gathered into a community of faith. And the "mission" must be a foreign, extraneous thing in any culture. The only things that will live will be churches of the people, by the people, and for the people; not of missionaries, by missionaries, and for missionaries.[26]

—James G. Van Buren

* * * * *

1. You are a member of the missions committee for your local church. Your congregation has observed the practice of designating the church's giving to missions, specific missionaries, or mission works rather than through a large national agency or denominational board. Upon what basis, then, will your committee determine which appeals for your funds should be granted? What missionaries will receive your regular support?

2. Your church has a strong program of mission education through the Bible school, youth, men's and women's groups, regular worship service emphases, an annual missions fair, and other projects. Upon what basis do you determine what missions and missionaries you will promote? What standards does your congregation or denomination have for its missionaries? What are their qualifications?

What must they accomplish to be worthy of your attention?

3. When you pray for your missionaries, what do you pray for?

4. What percentage of the total giving to a church should be designated for "missions"? How did you arrive at that figure?

5. Whose business is it to educate the church concerning missions and missionaries?

6. Many congregations delegate missions to the women's society. Why is this a dangerous practice? Or is it?

7. What is the purpose of your church's missions program? Do you have a well-defined strategy you are following for promoting church growth throughout the world?

8. Are your missionaries church-growth minded? Do their reports indicate a burning desire to win souls to Jesus Christ and establish congregations which can soon be independent of foreign domination?

9. Are your missionaries team-oriented, working in cooperation with others, or are they totally independent?

10. What standards have you developed to judge the effectiveness of your mission-dollar stewardship?

33: A CHECK LIST FOR SELECTING MISSIONARIES

Assuming that most mission activities are "good works," but also realizing that our mission dollars are limited, we expect missionaries supported by this congregation to meet the following church growth criteria:

1. Missionary is fully prepared for his task.
   ___ Adequate Bible education and personal Christian commitment
   ___ Specialized preparation in anthropology, linguistics, the culture of his field
   ___ Sufficient preparation in his homeland to test his endurance, judgment, adaptability on the field
   ___ Screening by a qualified medical doctor
   ___ Testing by a sympathetic but objective team of psychiatrists or psychologists
   ___ Knowledge of church growth research

2. Missionary is responsible to a governing board of directors (society or denominational board, elders of a local congregation, etc.).
   ___ He makes regular reports on the nature of his work and expects guidance in return.
   ___ He submits complete, audited financial statements no less than annually.
   ___ He expects on-the-field visits by members of his governing board for counseling, fellowship and encouragement.
   ___ He works as a team member assisting his fellow-workers whenever possible to accomplish mutually determined goals, the primary one of which is church planting.

3. Missionary maintains close ties with his supporting congregation.
   ___ Through regular newsletters
   ___ Through furlough visits
   ___ Through answers to occasional requests from the committee

4. Missionary is first and foremost an evangelist.
   ___ His first goal is to plant churches.
   ___ He is himself an evangelist or works closely in a supportive role with an evangelist.
   ___ He can demonstrate how his specific task is directly related to planting churches.
   ___ If his work fails to yield results, he is prepared to change tactics or locations if necessary.

5. Missionary has a right to expect from his supporting congregation:

___ Regular, personal, intercessory prayer

___ Regular, consistent financial support

___ Intelligent understanding of the nature of his field and his work

___ Letters of encouragement and counsel

___ Full fellowship as a member of the church

Chapter 8
THE MISSION DOLLAR: WHERE SHOULD IT GO?

No major business can survive today without careful management, cost-accounting procedures, continual checking of results against goals, and constant research and development. Although many persons hesitate to think of missions in this way, the modern missionary enterprise is a gigantic business. Annually hundreds of millions of dollars are spent on foreign missions. Thousands of missionaries and supporting personnel are employed by thousands of churches, societies, and agencies. A single mission board with hundreds of missionaries working in dozens of countries operates large accounting offices and promotional programs, oversees endowment funds and real estate holdings on the various continents, finances and staffs medical and educational institutions, delicately negotiates agreements with foreign governments, hires and fires laborers for construction of buildings, and all the rest of the multitudinous tasks involved in international business.

Churches, however, rest uneasy when their tasks are compared with business. Their purpose is to win souls to Jesus Christ as Lord, not to make money or develop real estate. Their primary concern in their financial dealings is that they exercise wise stewardship of the funds entrusted to them. They know that skilled money management alone cannot accomplish their task. Although they are frequently short of funds and must appeal to their constituencies for additional help, they know that prior to raising money they must ask and Scripturally answer, "Where should the money be used?" That is another way of asking, "What is the purpose of missions?"

History is replete with examples of churches, grown rich and lethargic, dying because they forgot their reason for being. For instance, Eugene Smith does not blame the seventh-century losses to Islam on the superior strength of the agressor alone. Rather, he says,

the defeats of the seventh century came to a church large in numbers, dominant in politics, powerful in leadership, rich in money, history, and intellect. The defeats came not alone because of outward threat, but in part because of inner spiritual weakness. That weakness was the failure of a great church to keep alive its sense of witness, to maintain a constant outreach in love, in the name of Jesus Christ, to its neighbors both near and far.[1]

When secondary matters usurped the priorities which called it into being, the church suffered enormous losses. It recovered only when it regained its sense of purpose, which is the motive for all foreign missionary undertakings.

That purpose, found in almost the same words in many church growth publications, is "to proclaim Christ and to persuade men to become His disciples and responsible members of His church." All other activities of the missions, no matter how noble in intent, are supportive at best. If they do not undergird this primary goal of discipling the lost, if they divert funds from discipling to support institutions at the expense of evangelism, then the secondary activities become genuinely subversive. Hence it is imperative, in church growth thinking, that priorities be determined in light of the divine commission. Only then can missionary leaders know where the money should go.

> *Wise administration by Church or Mission does not consist in blanket decisions to distribute resources according to long established percentages, paying no attention to, or even being ignorant of, the structure of church growth. Wise administration insists on being furnished with accurate knowledge of the degree, quality, nature, and probable future extent of church growth in each homogeneous unit or group of congregations. It then can make such choices as to methods, personnel, and distribution of resources as will achieve maximum growth.*[2]
> —Donald McGavran
> *How Churches Grow*

34: HOW IS THE MISSION DOLLAR SPENT?

Every dollar dedicated to foreign missions is divided into four unequal parts. The relative size of the four parts differs according to many variables: the prevailing philosophy of the sending body, the distance of the field from the sending country, the cost of living and other conditions on the field, the requirements of the home office, and so on. Every responsible church or society, however, includes these four items in its budget planning.

A. The missionary

Expenses for the missionary begin with his initial commitment to serve the Lord on the foreign field. He will pursue a specialized post-secondary education to prepare himself. Bible colleges or liberal arts college, seminary or graduate school, medical school, linguistics institute, aviation school—dozens of alternatives are available. Today's missionaries study for years to prepare themselves academically, culturally, psychologically, and spiritually for their task. Whether the money for this education is provided in part by the sending agency or the candidate assumes all this responsibility himself, his preparation remains the first expense.

Additional non-educational training may be required, such as in specialized camps (like those conducted by Wycliffe Bible Translators) or among different cultures in America (in city ghettoes, or among American Indians, for instance). Many boards see this training as essential preparation for the foreign field.

Almost all boards today require that missionary candidates be rigorously screened to determine their ability to adapt to a foreign culture and successfully pursue their ministry abroad. Medical and psychological tests, usually with in-depth clinical interviews, are commonplace. Further interviews with board committees and mission executives usually follow. In addition, candidates are encouraged to attend regional or national conferences on missions for further insight into their vocation.

All this intensive preparation is costly, yet mission leaders are convinced that stewardship demands that no costs be cut in the initial stages of a missionary's career. Wise investment of funds now can save unbearable losses later.

Once the missionary is approved by his sending agency and departs for his field (incurring other expenses, of course: transportation, passports and visas, shipping of luggage), his costs are relatively fixed. He needs his salary and field expenses, benefits (in medicine, education for children, retirement), repatriation fund, and other related items. A large part, therefore, of every missionary dollar is invested in the missionary's salary and expenses on the field.

MONEY AND THE MISSIONARY

It may at first sight seem strange to speak of finance as one of the external accompaniments of the preaching, rather than as part of the organization of the Church. But it is as it affects St. Paul's approach to his hearers that finance assumes its real significance and throws its most interesting light upon our missionary work today. The primary importance of missionary finance lies in the fact that financial arrangements very seriously affect the relations between the missionary and those whom he approaches. It is of comparatively small importance how the missionary is maintained; it is of comparatively small importance how the finances of the Church are organized: what is the supreme importance is how these arrangements, whatever they may be, affect the minds of the people, and so promote, or hinder, the spread of the Gospel.[3]

—Roland Allen
Missionary Methods:
St. Paul's or Ours?

* * *

At a gathering of the Evangelical Foreign Missions Association, T. Stanley Soltau of Korea made this statement: "I am convinced that the amount of foreign feeling can nearly always be expected in exact proportion to the amount of foreign funds used. The more foreign funds used in the work, the more anti-foreign sentiment you are likely to have."[4]

—Melvin L. Hodges
Growing Young Churches

B. The Home Base

The missionary's survival on his field, however, depends upon his supporting team in the sending country. A denominational missionary department, an interdenominational missionary agency, or perhaps a local church or group of churches has sent him to the field. A part of the missionary dollar, then, remains in the sending country to defray the expenses involved in serving the needs of the missionary. Administrative costs, usually ten to twenty-five percent of the annual budget for the home ministries staff, promotional costs (publications, prayer newsletters, etc.), and board expenses are necessary budget items in the supporting ministry of the sending agency.

C. The Field

In addition to the missionary's salary and personal expenses, costs are involved in operating and maintaining properties and institutions in the mission country. Medical and educational institutions, especially, are costly operations. Sometimes they are subsidized by the national governments of the countries; most often the bulk of the money comes from the sending country. In many countries, denominational missions are reducing their commitments to evangelism and Christian education in favor of these institutions, assuming that the former are the tasks which the young churches should incur without aid from abroad, but that they cannot manage the larger costs of the institutions. As we shall see, church growth leaders question that assumption.

MISSION PRIORITIES

Within the last 25 years missions have assigned the larger part of its missionary staff to institutional ministries, and our reason for doing so would no doubt be because of the demand in the spheres of education, literature, and medical work. However the church has been aware that we have given priority to these areas rather than to evangelism, Christian education, and church growth programs, and now they are following in the pattern of the mission. The best trained, even theologically, are being assigned to institutional programs rather than to strictly church ministries. One of the reasons is because of substantial and secure salaries that are available to them. We are creating a problem where institutions are going to be more important to them than the real functions of the

---

D. Research

This item always receives the smallest share of the missionary dollar, but most missionary societies realize its importance. No major industry can compete today without major efforts in research and development. Neither can modern missions. Louis J. Luzbetak's complaint may be somewhat more strongly stated than what others would like, but his basic sentiment is shared by all leaders in modern missions:

church. *Study by both the church and mission are urgently needed to rectify this.* [5]

—Sidney Langford
from *Missions in Creative Tension*

> Countless missionary years and lives are, humanly speaking wasted, and countless dollars are foolishly disposed of in the modern missionary effort because not enough research enters into missionary methods. Every industry has its team of research workers whose sole task is to discover more effective and more efficient ways of manufacturing and marketing the product in question. The Missions today needs few less salesmen and more research workers than are employed by this "industry." Mission research centers must be established with mission-minded specialists co-operating in every modern skill and scientific field. [6]

Church growth leaders would add that this research must keep solidly before it the goal of missions. In terms of dollars it asks, "How is the missionary dollar to be spent in order to cause the church to grow most effectively?"

This, then, is how the missionary dollar is apportioned. It must be a unified dollar: that is, each part must contribute to the whole. Unless missionary, home office, field operation, and research team agree upon the primary purpose of the mission, and work harmoniously to effect that purpose, the entire mission may collapse through internal dissention and increasing discouragement. Unless the building of the kingdom of God will yield to kingdom building by individual missionaries and mission executives, the church will not grow.

Full maturity in finances and propagation and government is a necessary Christian virtue, and has proved to be essential to church growth. In Korea, Burma, the South Pacific, and Uganda where there has been dramatic church growth, less foreign money has been spent in proportion to membership than in other mission fields of the world. There are sufficient church growth studies to show that when a church can take care of itself financially it is more relevant to its world, more evangelistic and missionary.[7]

—Louis L. King
from Missions in
Creative Tension

★ ★ ★

1. Since most missionaries and executives today agree to this apportioning of the missionary dollar, what distinguishes church growth thinking from that of more traditional mission thinking?

2. What about your home church? How is the dollar given to your church divided? Is it a "unified dollar," that is, with every part contributing to a common purpose? Who determines the budget? What is your church's purpose?

3. In order to operate more "economically" in periods of fiscal stress, several mission agencies have trimmed their budget in two places: missionary preparation and mission research. Discuss the effects these cuts could have on the long-range ministry of the agency.

4. Some of the fastest growing missions in the world today are not the wealthier, traditional missions, but the newer, poorer ones. What makes the difference? Is it possible that we Americans have placed too much emphasis upon money and too little on other, weightier matters?

35: TO WHAT FIELD DOES THE MONEY GO?

The previous unit discussed the most efficient use of the missionary dollar without raising a fundamental question of mission stewardship: to what field should the missionary dollar go? Since we have limited money and personnel, where can they most effectively be deployed? Since mankind's tenure on earth may be approaching its end, how can we disciple the largest numbers possible in the time left?

Jesus said, "The fields are white unto harvest." But some fields are whiter than others. Should they all be treated equally, hoping that all will eventually be won? Church growth thinkers believe that we cannot afford to practice gradualism any longer. As it has been previously defined, gradualism is dedication to carrying on activities which may slowly make their impact upon the consciences of men and communities so that in time men and women will be able to accept the Christian faith. Because the introduction of Christianity into a new country can usually be effected only gradually, this is the doctrine which prevails on new mission fields. The problem is that it often continues to dictate mission practices long after it has ceased to be useful. Gradualism may blind missionaries and young churches to the real possibilities for rapid growth or people movements. Gradualism has hidden from mission boards the fact that some peoples at any given time are more responsive than other peoples. Thus the sending agencies may continue to allocate resources by percentages based upon past allocations, rather than on current growth potential.

For years missionaries have been lauded for their sacrificial labor in unresponsive fields. Robert Bruce, a famed Irish missionary in Iran in the nineteenth century, established a work for the Anglicans among the Moslems. He says:

> I am not reaping the harvest; I can scarcely claim to be sowing the seed; I am hardly ploughing the soil; *but I am gathering out the stones.* That, too, is missionary work; let it be supported by loving sympathy and fervent prayer.[8]

Church growth thinkers have nothing but commendation for this spirit of humility and sacrifice and for the churches which have supported missionaries like Bruce through the years. But they insist that such gradualism cannot dictate the financing of missions today. If God has opened up a harvest field in Ethiopia among animistic peoples who are turning in large people movements to Christ, but has allowed the Moslems of Afghanistan to remain hardened against the gospel, then a mission board would be incompetent if it allocated its limited resources on an equal basis, fifty percent for Ethiopia and another fifty percent for Afghanistan.

The church growth school of thought has never advocated abandoning difficult fields. Realizing that a gradual approach is necessary in opening up new fields, it would not pull all missionaries out of difficult assignments with prospects for few conversions. It merely pleads that resources meet opportunities for growth wherever possible.

Donald McGavran illustrates proportionate financial assistance in missions in *Bridges of God*. After warning that policy should avoid both "fanatical devotion to self-support" which deprives converts of essential teaching "unless they pay for it" and "such short sighted paternalism that new congregations are indefinitely served, and hence ruled by foreign paid pastors," he urges us not to think in term of occupying territories but of assisting people movements.

> What then is the right standard of assistance? The answer is not a simple one. There are different degrees required for the various stages of People Movements. However, let us assume that the following standard of assistance had been adopted. It is partial, for several stages in People Movements are not even mentioned in it. It is highly simplified. But it will serve for illustration.
>
> Gathered colony churches—one missionary to each 3,000 souls.
> Completed People Movement churches—the same.
> People Movements of over 20,000 souls with unlimited opportunities for growth, a present rate of growth of 70 per cent per decade and as yet without a trained national ministry—one missionary to each 500 souls.
> People Movements like the above but with a trained national ministry—one missionary to each 1,000 souls.
> Young vigorous People Movements growing at the rate of 200 per cent a decade or more, numbering from 500 to 5,000 souls and located in the midst of a strategic people, with no higher trained national staff from among the incoming people—one to each 200 souls.[9]

—Donald McGavran
The Bridges of God

* * * * *

1. What fields does your church support? What have been the results? Why have you selected these fields?

2. Do you have a periodic review of the results of your evangelistic efforts in each field?

3. What is your reaction to Robert Bruce's justification of his efforts?

36: TO WHAT KIND OF "WORK" IS THE MONEY APPLIED?

The same principle of allocation which governs the selection of peoples to receive the missionary dollar determines to what aspect of the mission that dollar is applied. Schools, hospitals and clinics, teacher-preacher training institutes, ecumenical conferences, missionary and national evangelists, printers, radio stations, fraternal workers—all are good works, all need money. The church growth school of thought insists that the money go to assist those works which lead directly to the greatest growth for the church of Jesus Christ.

Many mission institutions should be generously supported; others should not. McGavran has defined three varieties of institutions. Their allotment of the resources becomes evident when they are compared:

> First, there are the institutions in advance of the Church—Christian hospitals in Arabia, Christian schools in Benares and other strongholds of Hinduism. Even evangelism carried on with a professional staff where very few if any become Christians becomes a kind of institution. The task of these enterprises is to stay alive, bearing as much witness to Christ as possible. It would be foolish to apply the criterion of church growth to them. They are successful if they just keep going. However, in view of the ever-increasing response to the Gospel, the number of such institutions grows less every passing year.

> Second, there are institutions dominating a non-growing Church. We think of the institutions in connection with younger Church Z of Chipania which had a membership of 4,890 in 1924 and 4,986 in 1954. It is now served by two hospitals, eighteen grade schools or parts of them, four high schools, one college, and one theological seminary. These absorb 92 per cent of the missionary assistance given to the Church, and 78 per cent of the budget. . . .

> Third, there are institutions serving a growing Church. Here the institution is justified by its growing churches. The schools of a flourishing Church to which come boys from 100 congregations are essential parts of the growth process. So are the hospitals and other auxiliary institutions. Those exposed to their influence go out into ripe populations.[10]

The effectiveness of this third group of institutions is measured by the church growth which these institutions help to achieve. With these three groups in mind, the mission board can determine which institutions it wishes to underwrite and in what proportions. Most older boards feel compelled to maintain a witness ministry in difficult fields, so they will continue to offer limited support to the first group. Most boards are entangled with institutions like those in group two; those operating on church growth principles will find ways to minimize or eliminate this involvement, hopefully by finding ways to turn them into institutions like those in the third group.

HEY DONOR AGENCIES: DON'T IMPOSE WESTERN FASHIONS ON US,
by Eight Officers of the Evangelical Church Mekane Yesus, Ethiopia

In January, 1971, the 7th General Assembly of the Evangelical Church Mekane Yesus, of Ethiopia passed a resolution requesting the Lutheran World Federation to ask Donor Agencies in Germany and other countries to reconsider their criteria for aid and include direct support for evangelism, congregational work, leadership training and church building. The Church realized her own inability to cope with the fast growing congregational work and the opportunities for evangelistic outreach. Over the last several years the Mekane Yesus Church has worked out development projects which meet the criteria decided by the Donor Agencies. At the same time, the Church in faithfulness to her Lord realized her obligation to proclaim the Gospel to ever growing crowds expecting more than bread. She cannot remain silent where genuine spiritual need is prevailing and thousands are flocking to newly established churches (and also in places where there are no churches) to hear the GOOD NEWS.

It has become evident over the last few years that the Churches and Agencies in the West are prepared to assist in material development, but have little interest in helping the Church meet her primary obligation to proclaim the Gospel. From the African point of view, it is hard to understand this. We question whether the criteria for assistance laid down by Donor Agencies are correct . . . In our view, a one-sided material development is not only self deceiving in the sense that man needs more than that, it is also a threat to the very values which make life meaningful, if carried out without due attention to simultaneously meeting spiritual needs . . . When we are told, by virtue of the criteria unilaterally devised by the Donor Agencies what we need and what we do not need, what is good for us and what is not good, we feel uncomfortable. . . .

Man's basic need is not simply to be informed of what is good and right. Man's primary need is to be set free from his own self-centered greed. Here is where the Gospel of the Lord Jesus Christ comes in as the liberating power . . . The need of the whole man (which includes his spiritual need as primary) should determine where assistance should be given, and not criteria laid down by the Donor Agencies which reflect trends in Western Societies and Churches. . . .

It has been falsely thought that the old emphasis in the mission of the Church had been solely on verbal proclamation and that the new emphasis on social action, community development, liberation from dehumanizing structure, and involvement in national building was now essential. The West has assumed that in the past missions have not paid due attention to the material and physical needs of man and have been concerned only for souls, doing little to bring about changes in society . . . This false assumption distorts the true picture. It is caused, not by a sober analysis of the historical facts, but by the dismay and feeling of guilt which gripped the Western Churches when, about twenty years ago, the injustice and exploitation of colonialism began to come to the surface. Western Churches began to ask themselves, "Have we been instruments of oppression? Have we been so busy saving souls, that we have ignored the social and political needs of man?" As the Churches rocked under the impact of such guilt (always implied as a sin of omission, even when the facts were contrary) the cry went up "Minister to the Whole Man." Certainly the missions have always emphasized medical work, education, and other community improvements, but in the sixties the Donor Agencies thought it necessary to make all such work highly visible to refurbish the 'mission image' in the sending countries. Even though such a division of ministry and witness was, from a theological point of view, indefensible.

This over reaction and sense of guilt on the part of the wealthy Western Churches led to a new imbalance in assistance to the younger Churches. All this happened in the West: but should developments in the West be the only determining factor in the aid relationship?

The Mekane Yesus Church in Ethiopia feels the time has come to call the attention of the Lutheran World Federation to this issue. It is our firm conviction that assistance should be brought into balance . . . The division between proclamation and development which has been imposed on us is, in our view, harmful to the Church and will result in a distorted Christianity.

Our hope is that our sister Churches do not judge our needs solely on their own criteria and on the conditions they have stipulated. We want to proclaim Christ because we believe it is

*our responsibility. We want to proclaim Christ because our
people are hungering for Him.*

Signed by Eight Officers of the
Evangelical Church Mekane Yesus,
Emanuel Abraham, Fitaurari Baissa Jammo, Emmanuel Gebre Silassie,
Osmund Lintjorn, Menkir Esayas, Olav Saeveraas, Berhe Beyene,
Gudina Tjmsa Gen. Sec.[11]

The above call for reevaluation of support to institutions was issued in January 1971.

The determination of these men to proclaim Christ to their hungering countrymen is a reaction against more than a century of well-
intentioned mission witness which placed as much faith in the
achievements of Western civilization as it did in the gospel of Jesus
Christ. Lord Macaulay, although not a missionary, in a letter from
India to his father on October 12, 1836, summarizes this faith in
"civilization":

> It is my firm belief that, if our plans of education are followed up,
> there will not be a single idolator among the respectable classes in
> Bengal thirty years hence: and this will be effected without any effort
> to proselytize—merely by the natural operation of knowledge and
> reflection.[12]

Macaulay's optimism was unfounded, of course, but nineteenth-
century missionaries did not know that. So many fine schools, as
well as other institutions, were founded to enlighten and correct the
lost. Time has proved this approach to conversion to be wrong.

> Careful investigation and research need to be done on all of our
> institutional work to determine which contribute to the growth of the
> church and how much. In the light of such investigations, it should be
> decided where man power and money power would be best used to
> advance the cause of Christ. Such investigation would prevent "the
> tail from wagging the dog" as seems to be the case so often today.
> Instead, institutions should be allowed to exist only as they contribute
> significantly to the growth of the church.[13]

—Sidney Langford
from *Missions in
Creative Tension*

* * * * *

1. How can the effectiveness of institutions be measured? Some would ask, "Aren't they good in themselves, needing no other defense?"

2. McGavran writes: "Most missions have spent most of their budget for nonevangelistic activities connected with lifting and changing society. They are doing this today and will do it tomorrow. The passion to perfect dominates most missions."[14] To church growth thinkers, McGavran is illustrating a flaw in mission administrative thinking. To other mission leaders, he is describing a virtue. What do you think?

37: SHOULD MONEY BE GIVEN DIRECTLY TO THE NATIONAL CHURCH?

With the growth of national churches in many lands, serious students of missions are now asking whether missions as such should not be phased out of those lands, with the mission dollar going directly to the national church leadership for allocation. George W. Peters outlines the three principles which have prevailed in this question and then gives his evaluation:

1. No foreign funds have been made available to national churches. This is the extreme application of the self-support principle under the label of indigenization. Due to this practice, there are today thousands of small, impotent, ill-cared-for, anemic groups of believers in the world struggling for survival. There is as much peril in undersupply as there is in over-supply of foreign funds. Balance and common sense are much needed in this matter.

2. Foreign funds are made available to the churches conditionally. Usually such provisions are made upon the recommendations of the missionaries and for projects approved by the missionaries. The missionary thus becomes the mediator between the churches and the board and the administrator of the funds.

3. Foreign funds are made available directly to the churches and without any conditions. Usually such allowances are made in a lump sum to be used in special projects or in programs as the church deems advisable. The national church renders a careful account of the appropriations of the funds, but administers them independently.

As in other matters so also here, there should be no unilateral decision in the area of foreign finances. Partnership in equality and mutuality must prevail. Dollar diplomacy has no more place in Christianity than nationalism has. It takes as much grace to give humbly as to receive proudly, to give without a sense of condescension as to receive without losing one's own self-hood and not to acquire a habit of expectation.

Perhaps nowhere do we need the mind of Christ as fully as in money matters in order not to offend Christian principles, not to retard the cause of Christ, remain indigenous (in the economic patterns of the land), build spiritual relationships as well as sound economic foundations and express real brotherhood concern and unity. Within genuine partnership there is no reason why churches which are economically strong should not contribute the larger share in the mission outreach and expansion of the church through aggressive evangelism. This certainly would not violate indigeneity or harm a spiritually minded church in her maturation process or the development of her self-respect, identity and sense of responsibility.

Sharing is as much a biblical principle as training in stewardship. Both aspects should be evident in partnership.

In general budgeting should proceed according to the following guidelines:

. . . All finances must be negotiated within the legislative body, duly considering needs and resources;

. . . All available finances must be prayerfully allocated in the light of the purpose of the church and according to biblical priorities;

. . . Only in exceptional and emergency cases should foreign funds be made available to continuing programs except evangelism and church expansion in which mission and church are unified. Foreign funds may be applied to special projects and to special missions;

. . . Funds must be responsibly administered under the authority of the legislative body and in keeping with the negotiated budget and purpose and according to the agreed upon projects;

. . . Responsible accounting must be rendered through the legislative body to the constituency which supplies the funds.

It may sound reasonable that money given to the Lord's work is the Lord's money and that the Holy Spirit has the right to disburse such money anywhere He leads and deems wise. Such emphasis is, however, only one side of the coin. Biblical stewardship does not only obligate to give unto the Lord the portion that belongeth unto Him. It also obligates to responsible administration. Responsible investment is an important aspect of biblical stewardship. The giver has a right to know how his money is being invested and administered. In stewardship mutual confidence does not exclude personal responsibility and accountability.[15]

38: HOW CAN WE KNOW WHERE THE
MONEY SHOULD GO?

The foregoing units have attempted to show that missions budgets should be constructed on the basis of these principles:

1. **A somewhat narrowly defined purpose for the mission:** Is it to do "good works"? To educate the illiterate? To heal the sick? To be a Christian witness? To alleviate social suffering? To proclaim Jesus Christ as Lord and win disciples for His church?

2. **A clearly developed worldwide strategy.** The mission board needs a strategy which sends missionaries where responsive peoples are ready. The strategy may involve gradualism, but must concentrate on church growth and measure its program against the criterion.

3. **A willingness to change the strategy when necessary.** Church growth leaders contend that a prime deterrent to growing conversions is missionary immobility. Immobility keeps missionaries where their work is no longer fruitful, institutions where they are stifling church growth, and mission budgets based upon the priorities of a decade ago.

4. **A strong sense of stewardship.** This is the Lord's money we are handling. Where and how can it be used most efficiently to glorify His name and strengthen and increase His church?

5. **A healthy respect for the nationals.** James A. Scherer reminds us that condescension is as much an evil as coercion.

> The nineteenth-century emphasis on moral and cultural uplift through missions was just as dangerous a displacement of the apostolic ideal as was the political motive. A clearly identifiable evil, coercion, gave way to a less palpable one, condescension. Missionaries came to the lands of Asia and Africa as representatives of a higher social order, convinced of the superiority of western civilization. Love for the sinner for whom Christ died degenerated easily into pity for the unfortunate and the backward. "Ourselves as your servants for Jesus' sake" was not the dominant missionary image. The disparity between the missionary's economic and educational standards and those of the people to whom he came led to paternalism both as an attitude and as a missionary method. Often the appeal to become Christians was based less on the Word of God than on prudential considerations. The special advantages of membership in the Christian community were commended to the inquirer. The aroma of Christ was strangely contaminated with the odor of self-

interest. The preaching of "Christ crucified" was often reduced to the offer of material inducements and the promise of social advancement. Sin was easily confused with social backwardness, and grace with progress and modernity. Christian life was presented as a higher form of culture and morality, access to which was gained by Christian education.[16]

Condescension perpetuates institutions and activities done "in behalf of" the less fortunate instead of allowing them to grow in grace and knowledge and independence. Churches do not grow where missionaries approach nationals as superiors to inferiors.

6. **A genuine confidence in the church to change lives and societies.** In studying the Indian situation, Bishop Pickett found that "there appears on the records a close relation between the preaching of the Gospel to the poor and (1) profession of faith by the poor, (2) the measure of moral, social and economic improvement achieved by the poor, and (3) the influence exerted by Christian converts from the poor upon non-Christians in the neighborhood."[17] That is why it is important that churches grow. Service institutions can never replace the church, but churches may use institutions to serve their entire communities.

* * * * *

1. A large element in American foreign policy since World War II has been our generous aid program. Americans have been puzzled, however, that often our dollars have not purchased friendship, but resentment, hostility, and cries of "Americans, go home!" The church has been equally surprised to find its paternalism in missions budget receiving similar results. As sympathetically as possible, place yourself in the recipient's place and explain this resentment.

2. In Europe many national churches are supported by taxes. In the United States all churches are supported with voluntary contributions. Where are the more active congregations? Why? What does this fact teach us about the use of our dollars on the mission field?

PART V

CONTEMPORARY ISSUES
AND CHURCH GROWTH

Several issues vie for the attention of church planners and mission leaders today. The emergence of strong nationalistic tendencies among developing countries, with former colonies casting off the control and influence of imperialistic powers; the continuing drive for world domination by communistic countries; the impact of Western materialism and scientism; the more popular social concerns like the war against poverty, the fight against pollution, and the struggle for racial equality, command the best intellectual efforts world leaders can give them. In such a complexity of causes, what priority should be given to church growth? Can missions ignore these challenges to traditional Christian thought? Is it sufficient to talk about "church-planting" in an era erupting with revolutions?

To give an example of church growth's position in relation to modern challenges, the following chapters will consider two problems: the role of Christianity among the world's religions, and the church growth attitude toward revolution. When the Christian faith is compared with the world's great religions, does it have a distinctive individuality which must be preserved and propagated in a pluralistic society? With revolutionaries calling for an abandoning of traditions and the formation of totally new civilizations, where is the place of the church to be found? As church growth thinking answers these questions, it gives evidence of its general position on the other major issues of contemporary society.

Chapter 9
CHRISTIANITY AND WORLD RELIGIONS

This chapter raises a vital question: how should Christianity relate itself to the other religions of the world? Unit 39 explores some of the answers the Christian faith can give to this question.

Units 40 and 41 examine, in more detail, three *typical* positions which have existed and are still existing today. The units explore the attitudes of Karl Barth and Hendrik Kraemer and the posture of "Joint Search" toward non-Christian religions. The discussion moves from the most to the least exclusive in the relationship between Christianity and non-Christian religions.

Historically, Kraemer's *The Christian Message in a Non-Christian World* prepared for the Madras Conference of 1938 was a response to *Rethinking Missions* (1932) by the Laymen's Commission. The main architect of the Laymen's Report was William E. Hocking of Harvard, who later elaborated his position in *Living Religions and a World Faith* (1940). The so-called Hocking-Kraemer debate of 1938 serves as an archetype of the discussion of the relationship of the gospel and non-Christian religions. Much has been written since then, but the issues surrounding the Hocking-Kraemer debate are timeless and still provide points of concern for church growth today.

Units 42 and 43 examine the strategic (rather than theological and philosophical) understanding of the religions.

39: A THEOLOGICAL PENDULUM

Donald McGavran, in the following selection, brings out representative theological understandings of these world religions. While reading this essay, you will want to ask yourself the following questions: What is the proper relationship of Christianity to non-Christian religions? What does the Bible have to say about this subject? What is your own conviction? Imagine yourself to be a missionary trying to convey Christ's message of salvation to people living in a predominantly non-Christian world. Place yourself in the same position in your own country.

* * * * *

A hundred years ago as Christians stood beside the grave of the King of Ashanti and saw 500 wives killed and buried with him—as an act not of savagery but of high religion, through a sincere and reasoned preoccupation with the world to come; as they saw millions of goats, roosters, and pigs sacrificed squealing to various gods and goddesses in India; as they observed the grip of religious cannibalism in Oceania, they said frankly that non-Christian religion was all wrong. The pendulum, let us say, was at the far right.

WHICH OF THE FOLLOWING STATEMENTS COMES CLOSER TO YOUR OWN POSITION? EXPLAIN.

—NON-CHRISTIAN RELIGIONS ARE ALL WRONG. CHRISTIANITY POSSESSES THE ONE AND ONLY REVELATION OF GOD TO MAN.

—ALL RELIGIONS ARE EQUALLY TRUE OR EQUALLY GOOD.

About fifty years ago at the turn of the twentieth century, Christian Missions had purged non-Christian religions of their grossest elements. Through the activities of orientalists, missionaries, and men like Raja Ram Mohun Roy and Vivekananda, many hidden excellencies came to light. Non-Christian religions, met in their high scriptures, were found to have many good qualities and sublime insights, much sound common sense and wisdom for living. The pendulum now swung to the far left. Non-Christian religions began to be counted wonderful, true, and good.

> **GIVE FIVE EXAMPLES OF "NON-CHRISITAN RELIGIONS" AND A BRIEF DESCRIPTION OF EACH. DOES YOUR DEFINITION OF RELIGION INCLUDE SCIENTISM, MARXISM, NIHILISM, AMERICAN SECULARISM, OR AGNOSTICISM?**

A school of thought held that as Christianity used the scriptures of the Jews for Old Testament, Christianity today might use the Hindu, Confucian, and Buddhist writings as its current Old Testament. Furthermore, just as Christianity adopted the philosophy of the Greeks, so it might adopt the philosophy of Shankara Acharya, the great Hindu Monist, or enrich itself with the devotional and disciplinary wealth of Buddhism. . . .

[In 1932] the Laymen's Commission brought out its famous report. Hocking's frank advocacy of shared search for truth with sister religions —all inspired by God—as the right missionary method for all future time was very much a piece with a great deal of missionary thinking. I remember hearing it ardently defended by a United Church of Canada missionary at a meeting of the Mid-India Christian Council.

> **WHAT DOES "SHARED SEARCH FOR TRUTH WITH SISTER RELIGIONS" MEAN TO YOU?**

This swing of the pendulum is far from over. Indeed, it has been given a strong additional push farther to the left by the natural religion of our current pluralistic society. Pluralistic society gravitates to religious relativism. When your four closest neighbors are respectively Roman Catholic, Buddhist, Marxist, and Mormon; and you find them all good people, who loan you their lawn mowers and give you a lift when your car won't start, it is natural to conclude "They have their religions and I have mine. Theirs is good for them and mine for me." This is religious relativism. It permeates all thinking today. . . .

> **DEFINE PLURALISTIC SOCIETY. IS PLURALISTIC SOCIETY SYNONYMOUS WITH RELIGIOUS RELATIVISM? WHAT IS RELIGIOUS RELATIVISM?**

Another force pulling the pendulum to the left is the sceptical mood of great numbers of the educated. They have graduated from Christianity, but are not anti-religious. They regard religions of all sorts as useful adjustments reached by various societies. They believe life is more harmonious and satisfying when lived *as if* some religion were true. Not that it really is. God is not real. There is no future life. Sin is not a useful social concept; but it is a good thing to send the children to Sunday School and be a member of the Church or mosque. One should support all these civic enterprises. Since all religions have only instrumental value, are only relatively true, they are all essentially false, of course.

The cold war pushes the pendulum still farther left. America needs allies. We must not offend the nations of Africasia. We must court them. Since religion is a sensitive point—so the argument runs—we must assure them that their religion is just as good as ours. The *Reader's Digest* is not a profound magazine, but it does reflect popular tastes. A couple of years ago it carried an article by Michener—later of fame as the author of *Hawaii*—telling what wonderful people Moslems are and what a wonderful religion they have. An article in a recent *Christian Century* affirms that college students today are much interested in comparative religions.

THE IMPACT OF PLURALISTIC SOCIETY, THE SCEPTICISM OF THE EDUCATED, AND THE COLD WAR ARE CITED AS FORCES PULLING THE PENDULUM TO THE LEFT. CAN YOU THINK OF OTHERS?

The net result of all this is an exceeding great tenderness toward other religions—as if the chief Christian problem was that of not offending adherents of other faiths. Instead of which, a chief problem today is how Christians, at every level, can keep from being overwhelmed by relativism. In this post-Christian world, relativism gets at us from every angle—often when we are entirely unconscious of it.

. . . Pluralistic society generates relativism like a rocket generates flame. This all-embracing relativism or "truth indifferentism" is the great new fact of our time to which we must address ourselves when we consider the Gospel and non-Christian religions.

FACED WITH "THE GREAT NEW FACT OF OUR TIME," WHAT IN YOUR OPINION CAN THE CHURCH DO TO EFFECTIVELY PROCLAIM CHRIST?

Yet we keep talking as if the pendulum were at the right end of its swing. We keep insisting that we must not attack other religions. I have been a missionary for thirty-eight years. I never heard any Christian (missionary or national) attack another religion. Christians are busy proclaiming Christ and serving men. They tell of God's gracious goodness in becoming man for us and our salvation. They tell of Christ's sacrificial death on the cross that we through faith on Him might be saved. They announce that in Christ's resurrection, God broke the power of sin and death. Believe me, Christians attacking other religions are a figment of our imaginations. Attack is not our problem. Our problem is relativism.

We keep insisting that there are valid insights in other religions. Who denies it? Our problem is not Christians stridently denying that other religions have some good, just, and sublime insights in them. Our problem is Christians who seriously believe that *all* other religions are ways to God, confer salvation just as truly as the Christian faith, and are as good for their adherents as Christianity is for us. This is where the pendulum hangs today.[1]

—Donald McGavran

40: BARTH AND KRAEMER LOOK AT NON-CHRISTIAN RELIGIONS

The Position of Barth and Early Kraemer.

Karl Barth and Hendrik Kraemer, in his early writing,[2] stress the impotence of man to find or understand God. Man's speculation or discovery is man's wisdom, which is the partial transitory conclusion of finite man. In God's plan of salvation He has revealed himself in Israel and supremely in Christ. Barth writes:

> The Bible is the concrete medium by which the Church recalls God's revelation in the past, is called to expect revelation in the future, and is thereby challenged, empowered, and guided to proclaim.[3]

The Bible attests past revelation only when it speaks to us and is heard by us as God's Word. What Barth means by attestation is "to point in a definite direction beyond oneself to something else."[4] Then, it follows that the Bible gives authoritative witness as it lets *that something else* be the authority, that is, God's revelation thus attested. The revealed Word of God is the Word God spoke to the prophets and apostles in Jesus Christ, and still speaks through their instrumentality to men of today. The church's *kerygma* (proclamation) is "ventured upon in recollection of past, and in expectation of future revelation."[5] Barth is saying that *kerygma* is spoken in recollection, that in the historical event of Jesus Christ, God has already spoken once and for all. It is at the same time heralded in expectation that God will disclose himself to those who receive the message. Thus Christ, His only revelation, is discontinuous with all "other" religions or faiths. The mission of the church, then, is to bring men to Christ, who is the only way to salvation.

Kraemer shares much the same view as Barth.

The Position of Later Kraemer.

Kraemer in his later writings[6] softens his temper toward other religions, but still maintains that man by himself cannot find or understand God. He no longer holds the view of *total rejection*, that is, viewing Christ as being God's only revelation discontinuous with all other religions. His modified position is that God has been revealing himself from of old to all men in all religions, but he does not fail to mention that these revelations are greatly distorted by the finiteness and sinfulness of those religions and that the only undistorted revelation is found in and through Jesus Christ.

> What is absolute then is not Christianity but the Revelation of God in Jesus Christ. He has no need of our proofs. He simply reigns from the cross, even were no one to recognize the fact.[7]

This undistorted revelation of God has nothing to learn from the distortions of other religions. While he stressed the doctrine of discontinuity earlier, Kraemer now modifies it so that revelation is continuous in all religions as evidenced by man's effort to understand God. But he contends that there is a quality of revelation in Jesus Christ which is unique when compared with other religions. Therefore the followers of Christ must propagate the gospel to win men and nations.

Is there a substantial difference between early and later Kraemer? In what sense can you say Christianity is continuous with non-Christian religions and in what sense can you say it is not?

41: JOINT SEARCH FOR TRUTH

Unit 40 introduces two theological positions on the relation of Christianity to non-Christian religions. A third position may be categorized as "Joint Search for Truth." The attitude of appreciation and synthesis, expressed by the Laymen's Commission in 1932 and more particularly by William E. Hocking of Harvard, serves as a classic example of the third position. In the words of Hocking,

> **A.** Reconception is the way of a true *conservatism:* it conserves as much as possible of what is worth conserving in other faiths; it provides a permanent frame for all those scattered "accents of the Holy Ghost" which, treasured in local traditions here and there, are robbed by their separateness of their due force.[8]

What this statement means is that each religion should examine itself in the light of and with the cooperation of all other religions. It should endeavor unselfishly to serve mankind and diligently seek God, and then the blessed outcome will be the reconceiving of itself and the discerning of God's perfect revelation. Hocking's contention is that this revelation thus received is something similar to Christianity. Christians are urged to re-examine themselves, serve fellowmen, and seek God. They must learn what they can from other religions. Conversion from other faiths or the winning of men and nations ought to be of little concern to the Christian church.

> **B. Sri Ramakrishna, an educated holy man of India says: Different creeds are but different paths to reach the Almighty. Various and different are the ways that lead to the temple of Mother Kali at Kalighat. Similarly, various are the ways that lead to the house of the Lord. Every religion is nothing but one of such paths that lead to God ... It is one and the same Avatara that, having plunged into the ocean of life, rises up in one place and is known as Krishna, and diving down again rises in another place and is known as Christ.[9]**

More recently, emphasis has been laid on the dialogue-relationship between the various religions. The Division of Studies of the World Council of Churches sponsored a consultation at Kandy, Ceylon, from February 27—March 3, 1967. The Kandy Consultation produced a document titled "Christians in Dialogue with Men of Other Faiths" which includes the following statement describing the nature of such encounter.

C. Love always seeks to communicate. Our experience of God's communion with us constrains us to communion with men of other beliefs. Only so can the Christian live the "with-ness" which was shown him in the Incarnation. His intercourse takes the form of dialogue, since he respects the differences between him and others, and because he wishes to hear as well as to speak. The fundamental nature of dialogue is this genuine readiness to listen to the man with whom we desire to communicate. Our concern should not be to win arguments.

We believe that Christ is present whenever a Christian sincerely enters into dialogue with another man: the Christian is confident that Christ can speak to him through his neighbour, as well as to his neighbour through him. Dialogue means a positive effort to attain a deeper understanding of the truth through mutual awareness of one another's convictions and witness. It involves an expectation of something new happening—the opening of a new dimension of which one was not aware before. Dialogue implies a readiness to be changed as well as to influence others. Good dialogue develops when one partner speaks in such a way that the other feels drawn to listen, and likewise when one listens so that the other is drawn to speak. The outcome of the dialogue is the work of the spirit.[10]

D. Syncretism as a theological problem concerns not only missions but all serious theological thinking in this time of increasing contact among the great religions. In fact, it is one of the most universal theological problems in which is implied the understanding of Truth (in the religious and philosophical sense), its authenticity and the source of its authority. As a theological and (I would add) philosophical problem, syncretism is, or at any rate should be, one of the truly great problems in the East-West dialogue. But it is not merely theoretical. It is eminently practical because it decides the whole attitude of life and its directive ultimates.[11]

—Hendrik Kraemer

WORD STUDY:

reconception

revelation

conversion

Avatara

Krishna

incarnation

syncretism

* * * * *

1. In describing the position of later Kraemer (see Unit 40), we have stated his conviction that "there is a quality of revelation in Jesus Christ which is unique when compared to other religions." Then the basic difference between Christianity and other religions lies in kind rather than in degrees. How does Kraemer's position compare with Hocking's in Unit 41A? In your opinion, which position is more likely to foster church growth? Why?

2. Is the concept of religious relativism contained in paragraph B prevalent in America? Among your friends? Consider the following expressions:
   a. "It doesn't matter which path you take. You will eventually reach the top of the mountain."
   b. "All roads lead to God."
   c. "Trying to convert others to your religion is not justified. After all, how can you be sure that yours is right?"
   d. "Every religion has some good in it. The important thing is to live up to it."
   e. "All religions are right in their own way."

3. Give a brief paragraph (certainly no more than 100 words) or even a single sentence *definition of "dialogue with other faiths."*

4. Kraemer in paragraph D says that syncretism is a problem. Syncretism refers to the synthesizing of divergent world views and belief systems which results in the birth of a new thought pattern. Suppose someone were to argue for the justification of syncretism from the historical survey. In the first century, he would argue, there is evidence that the Christian religion received much from non-Christian sources. The Egyptian, Medianite, Canaanite, and Babylonian sources contributed much to the religion of the Old Testament. Christian faith is a fulfillment rather than a radical displacement of Judaism. He may further point to the common elements of paganism and Christianity in the subsequent history of the church. How do you make your defense, if such is your desire? If, however, you support the justification of syncretism, ask yourself: While there is much evidence in the first century that Christianity had some Hellenistic and Judaic influence, did such influence lead Christians to the point of questioning the truth of the Christian message?

42: CHRIST THE WAY

Thomas said to him,
"Lord, we do not know where you are going;
how can we know the way?"

Jesus said to him,
"I am the way,
and the truth,
and the life;
no one comes to the Father, but by me.

If you had known me,
you would have known my Father also;
henceforth you know him and have seen him"
(John 14:5-7, RSV).

CHRIST THE WAY?
THE WAY TO WHAT?

Do Churchmen believe the uniqueness of Christ? Many evidences indicate that as nations draw closer together, not merely in space and time, but more significantly in mind and spirit, syncretism of religions will become more and more attractive. Christian missions will be tempted to become less and less the proclamation of a unique Savior. What churchmen believe about Christ is crucial. Do they really believe Him when He says, "no man cometh unto the Father but by me"?[12]

—Donald A. McGavran
How Churches Grow

Examine Bible commentaries on John 14:5-7. Are there notable differences of interpretation among them?

Review the theological positions of Barth and Kraemer and contrast them with the posture of "Joint Search." Which position is most capable of preserving the uniqueness of Christ?

He who declared "I am the way, and the truth, and the life; no one comes to the Father, but by me" would not settle for less than being that way, that truth, and that life. And if Christ had believed that other ways, truths, and lives would eventually lead people to the ultimate goal, would He have said this in the first place, and further commanded His disciples to "go and preach" the message of salvation? Is there any need of our taking up His cross and following Him for any particular reason, if there are many paths through which one can reach this destination? What about the devout Hindus and Buddhists? The true and honest confrontation of Christianity with non-

Christian religions takes place only when we examine the differences, instead of similarities, that exist between them. What do you think about all this?

* * * * *

SELECT ONE VOLUME FROM THE BOOK LIST AND WRITE A THREE-PAGE DOUBLE-SPACED CRITICAL REVIEW BY INCORPORATING THE FOLLOWING QUESTIONS.

1. From what point of view is the book written? State in a sentence or two the major thesis of the book.
2. Does the author make his point adequately? Evaluate the extent to which the author succeeds in substantiating his thesis.
3. Do you agree with the author? If so, why? If not, why not?
4. Has the author influenced your thinking? If so, in what way?
5. What church growth insights have you received from the reading?

Ashby, Philip H. *The Conflict of Religions.* Scribner's, 1955.
Bouquet, A. D. *The Christian Faith and Non-Christian Religions.* Harper, 1958.
Dewick, E. C. *The Christian Attitude to Other Religions.* Cambridge, 1953.
Farquhar, J. N. *The Crown of Hinduism.* Oxford, 1920.
Forman, Charles W. *A Faith for the Nations.* Westminster, 1957.
Kraemer, Hendrik. *Why Christianity of All Religions?* Westminster, 1962.
Neill, Stephen. *Christian Faith and Other Faiths.* Oxford, 1961.
Perry, Edmund. *The Gospel in Dispute.* Doubleday, 1958.
Smart, Ninian. *A Dialogue of Religions.* SCM, 1960.
Stewart, William. *India's Religious Frontier.* Fortress, 1964.
Tillich, Paul. *Christianity and the Encounter of the World Religions.* Columbia, 1961.

43: A STRATEGIC VIEW OF RELIGIONS

An abundance of literature deals with the relation of Christianity to non-Christian religions from theological and philosophical perspectives. The Christian World Mission is yet to see a comprehensive treatment of this subject from a strategic (church growth) point of view. The strategic understanding of the religions is one of the crucial issues facing Christian mission today and will remain so for decades to come. Therefore, research must be undertaken with the expressed goal of formulating church growth principles dealing with non-Christian religions. To be sure, some hard thinking is being done and preliminary guidelines are available. Make your own list of principles and guidelines which will sharpen the effectiveness of the gospel proclamation in the context of a non-Christian world.

1. Recognize the reality of religious mosaic. For example, Buddhism is a major religion in Japan along with Shinto, but these two are not the only religions existing in Japan. The Buddhism which spread to Japan from India is known as Mahayana Buddhism. Furthermore, within this brand of Buddhism there are six major schools of thought, each divided by sects and branches. One school of thought, Amida Buddhism, consists of five major sects with one of them divided into ten branches. Like Japan, every nation has one or more prevalent religions influencing the lives of its people. Thus some are Buddhists, others Hindus, and still others Muslims within one nation. Each of these religions has pieces and yet smaller chips depicting religious mosaic. Shearer stresses the importance of recognizing the mosaic in his study of Korean church growth.

> Not only must we study the doctrines and creeds of this people's religion, but we must also understand how it affects the person himself in this society. A study of Buddhist sacred writings alone is not sufficient, but we must know in addition the dynamic forces of a particular type of Buddhism on the people in a society, to understand their response or lack of it to the Gospel.[13]

Acknowledging those particular varieties within each religion which are responsive (or conversely resistant) to the gospel is a prerequisite to church growth.

2. Understand the growth process that a numerical increase of a religion occurs when converts are won from other religions. This numerical growth should not be confused with biological growth, that is, growth from within the same faith through the entrance into the church of the offsprings of the adherents. On the contrary, numerical growth refers to additions from the world, that is, growth obtained through the conversion of persons from other religions. This appears to be the universal pattern of the growth of any religion. McGavran says that

> the younger Churches are growing among peoples whose hereditary religions are something other than Christianity. Churches always grow by converting men from some other faith. Indeed, every faith grows by converting men from another system. Hinduism converted its hundreds of millions from prior faiths, drove out Buddhism, greatly diminished Jainism, and supplanted various forms of animism. Islam converted population after population in its spread. So it is with every faith, and so with Christianity.[14]

3. Consider the receptivity to the gospel of the nominal believers (Buddhists, Confucianists, or Shintoists in name only) in each variety of each religion. Of this receptivity Lamott states as follows:

> The great body of converts from the higher cultures have come from men and women upon whom the old faith has already lost its hold, who see in Christianity a positive, definite gospel to fill the vacuum left by the departure of the old.[15]

The Christian World Mission must view the multitude of religionists in name only as a definite category of people who stand in need of conversion to Christ.

4. Promote research in the identification and analysis of the varieties of non-Christian religions receptive to the gospel.

> **Instead ... of a study of Buddhism, Hinduism, or Islam, being made on a basis which treats each religion as a unit, schools of missionary preparation and theological seminaries of the younger Churches need to teach the faiths of mankind, attending specially to those varieties which respond to Christian teaching. What in the Confucianism of district Y makes Confucianists there turn to the Christian faith? That is the comparative religion of importance for Christians. It is almost entirely a virgin field.[16]**
> **—Donald A. McGavran**
> ***How Churches Grow***

a. Africasian missionary societies should create within them departments of research geared toward the investigation of responsive varieties.

b. Eurican churches should cooperate with Africasian churches by supplying missionary research associates (or fraternal workers trained in church growth) to carry out necessary research.

c. Theological seminaries of the "younger" churches and missionary training centers of Eurica should offer courses in church growth-oriented comparative religion.

d. Symposia dealing with "The Gospel and the Non-Christian Religions" should be promoted and maintained by the Christian World Mission. Such symposia must be planned with special attention to the reality of religious mosaic. The proceedings of the symposia should be published.

Chapter 10
CHURCH GROWTH AND REVOLUTION

It has become commonplace to refer to the twentieth century as an age of revolution. Change characterizes every aspect of contemporary civilization. Governments rise and fall with an increasing tempo. The impacts of Marxism, various shades of nationalism, Western materialism, and instant communication have transformed cultural patterns in every continent on the globe. So rapid have been these changes that certain sociologists speak of "future shock," and a new breed of social scientists who call themselves "futurologists" has recently emerged.

These thinkers warn that there is no way to retard the acceleration of change. Today's solutions cannot answer tomorrow's problems. To such thinkers, it is anachronistic for the venerable church to totter into the future with missionary programs based upon the nineteenth- and early twentieth-century experience. A revolutionary world calls for revolutionary action. To speak of evangelism or church planting or personal salvation is to betray a failure to understand the times. In a world come of age the church must roll up its sleeves and work vigorously for the revolution of the whole society. The church can no longer be a gathering of Christians out of the world; it must become a dispersion of individuals infiltrating the power centers of society. Only thereby can inequality, poverty, discrimination, war, and every other social injustice be corrected. The Church must become an agent of change in a world that needs changing.

Church growth thought does not deny that ours is a revolutionary age. In fact, it points to cultural transitions as opportunities for evangelism and church planting. What it questions, however, is the role of the church as agent of revolutionary change. Is it the task of the church to transform society or individuals? Church growth leaders believe the church's divine task to be to bring individuals to a saving knowledge of Jesus Christ and incorporate them into the life of the congregation of believers. When this conversion has been accomplished, transformed persons will act as leaven on their society, thereby effecting changes in morality, government, and every other cultural phenomenon.

The missionary's responsibility, then, is not to be a social activist, agitating for political reform. His first responsibility is to evangelize and disciple in his area. In this role he will inescapably be an agent of change. Insofar as he is effective in communicating the gospel he will indirectly be responsible for far-reaching changes in his community. One has but to point to any country in which Christianity has become the faith of a people to demonstrate this fact. That as the established religion it has often become stagnant and unresponsive to human needs, or has too closely identified itself with the political and economic status quo, or is itself in need of renewal does not deny its history as a powerful revolutionary force.

On the following pages the various implications of today's revolutionary struggles are discussed in light of the church's responsibility. No conclusive answers are given—such conclusiveness is impossible in the midst of the struggle. The church growth commitment to the New Testament imperative to "disciple the nations" is apparent, however, even in the midst of change.

44: THE NATURE OF REVOLUTION

Ordinarily in the modern popular usage revolution has signified *political* revolution and has usually carried with it the idea of change by intentional and violent means. Increasingly, however, the term is coming to have a broader meaning that includes the kinds of rapid changes experienced today, which are more than political, are often not intended by anyone, and are not necessarily violent or illegal. The revolutionary changes of our times are certainly rapid and can involve sharp breaks with the past, but they are far more than political revolutions; they are changes in the very social fabric, in the material that governments seek to order. For this reason these changes are ordinarily more basic than those wrought by violence, though the changes at times may encourage violence or be furthered (or held back) by violence. Furthermore, the rapid changes of today suggest that we must include in the meaning of social revolution the possibility of changes much more extensive and thoroughgoing than ordinarily occur in brief periods of time—systemic changes, not simply revisions or reforms within an old and continuing order. Not all the changes we see are systemic changes, but the most basic changes may be. Systemic changes involve a wholesale transformation of the existing order and not simply modifications that can be contained within that order. To summarize, the term revolution has come to mean today the novel and not simply repetition, the possibility of change in the whole society and not simply in the personnel of the rulers or the forms of government, the rapid but not necessarily the violent change, and the possibility of thoroughgoing reshaping of the social system and not simply revising within that system.

As we try to understand more specifically the characteristics of the contemporary social revolution, we need to take special caution to avoid two very frequent errors. The first is the tendency to place simple moral tags on situations of rapid change. It is tempting to those who see the need for change in existing structures to believe that change is here and everywhere good, because it is change, and the more rapid and the more thoroughgoing, the better. Any such indiscriminate preference for change, however, involves not simply sympathy for the victims of the *status quo,* but also inability to appreciate the constructive roles of order and continuity and structure. The compulsive, the indiscriminate revolutionary eventually seeks to stamp out every remnant of the past because it is of the past. The indiscriminate revolutionary is in principle, whether in practice or not, the burner of libraries, the scorner of the learned, the persecuter of men of principle precisely because they have convictions, the destroyer of the identities of men and of civilizations. He is a barbarian, unable to find even an identity of his own that he wishes to preserve in the midst of the flux.

Nor is it any better to conclude that order and continuity are the only goods, always and everywhere to be preferred to change. Under a rigid social system men suffer differently, but just as painfully, as they do from indiscriminate change, and the changes that go on in spite of all efforts to the contrary simply build up frustration until their accumulation produces a violent upheaval. It is not appropriate to label rapid social change either good or evil *per se*. It is ambiguous. On the one hand rapid change always involves pain and suffering for at least some. Those who willingly seek the new therefore ought not ignore its evils. On the other hand rapid change provides opportunities to serve needs that previously were excluded from service. Those who seek to avoid the evils of rapid change ought not thereby condemn rapid change as such. The concern in this course, then, will hopefully be to understand better the changes of our time as a basis for more discriminating moral and intellectual judgments and responses.

A second frequent error in the interpretation of social change is the failure to see the interweaving of change with continuity. People in the midst of disruptive change are ordinarily so conscious of movement, often painfully so, that they may not be aware how much continuity with the past is still present. It takes a later generation of historians to point out, for example, how much the churches of the Reformation had in common with medieval Catholicism, or how significantly an industrialized and urbanized South resembles an earlier, agrarian South, or how much of pre-revolutionary Russia still endures to shape the life of the Soviet Union. However radical the changes, it is important that they not cause us to lose sight of significant continuities with the past. At the same time it is quite possible that such pervasive changes can occur that the social continuities that remain are much less important than usual. Even so the continuities can never be eradicated. In even so intensely change-conscious a society as that of contemporary Communist China, many things remain relatively impervious to human efforts: language, geographical location, climate, and ordinarily one's international neighbors, to mention a few. In human life we never encounter either pure change unrelieved by continuity or pure continuity untouched by change, nor would either be tolerable if it occurred. One churchman, commenting recently on the social revolution, wrote: "We are in the midst of a totally new civilization." (Harry O. Morton, in *The Student World,* No. 1, 1963, p. 45.) Now either that is conscious hyperbole or it is serious confusion. The "totally new" could not even be understood or communicated. About it one could not even say "totally new," but at best, "What was that?" There are no times of non-change, nor times of pure change, some of our stereotypes to the contrary. Instead we experience variations in the rate and extensiveness of change, in endless variety, but always mixed with continuities from the past.[1]

—Joseph L. Allen

* * * * *

1. Allen sees revolution as "the possibility of change in the whole society." We know that in social upheaval people are often open for changes of allegiance, in-

cluding religious belief. What does Allen's analysis say about the possibilities for real evangelism in today's world?

2. Why does Allen call the "compulsive, the indiscriminate revolutionary" a "barbarian"?

3. Explain Allen's warning against placing "simple moral tags" on rapidly changing situations. When is change "right"? When is it "wrong"?

4. Why is Morton wrong to talk of a "totally new civilization"?

5. Our world is exploding with revolutions—in Latin American countries, in Africa, in Asia. As Christian Americans, what should be our response to these upheavais?

6. Fife and Glasser *(Missions in Crisis,* p. 29) summarize today's revolutionary status this way: "The world is in revolutionary upheaval. Leaders are acutely aware of population trends, limited food supplies, the growing restlessness of the displaced farmers forming the new urban masses. These leaders continue to appeal to large nations, East and West, for economic aid. Their peoples must be settled and satisfied. Work and food must be provided. Industrialization and scientific farming must be introduced on a massive scale if there is to be any hope of future survival." What role does the church play through its missions in supplying these needs?

45: THE ROLE OF THE CHURCH IN REVOLUTION

A. In the first centuries

Of the processes by which Christianity spread in these five centuries, and especially in the first three, we have all too little information. Missionaries who, like Paul, made the propagation of the faith their main passion undoubtedly had a large part. Prophets and professional teachers also had a share. Probably individual lay folk did something incidental to their everyday tasks. An extensive apologetic literature may have reached some, either directly or indirectly, by providing arguments which could be employed orally. The public address and attendance on services were of assistance. Catechetical instruction and careful testing of applicants helped to insure intelligent comprehension, sincerity, and approximation to the ethical standards of the Christian community. During the first three centuries, conversion seems to have been chiefly by individuals and families. Always it was primarily individual change rather than the complete transformation of society which Christians envisaged—except as that latter was expected to come in cataclysmic fashion by the sudden act of God. Yet mass movements there were. Towards the close of the third century they came in Armenia and in parts of Asia Minor. Then, in the fourth century, the Roman state took an increasingly friendly attitude and eventually commanded compulsion in the destruction of the pagan religions. This brought millions into the Church, and often from very superficial motives and without much knowledge of any but a few outward formalities of the Christian cult, some of the ethical requirements, and a hope of an immortal life of happiness.[2]

The methods by which Christianity spread, then, often worked a revolution in the lives of individuals and gave rise to communities which sought in greater or less separation from society, to practice ideals which differed from those of the world. However, such general social results as followed were not planned, but were incidental to changes in individuals.[3]

—Kenneth Scott Latourette
The First Five Centuries

B. In European civilization

Precisely how far European peoples owed their later primacy to Christianity cannot be accurately determined. Clearly that faith was not the only factor. Clearly, too, much of the European hegemony was accompanied by developments such as African slavery and the intensification of the incidence and destructiveness of war which were quite contrary to the genius of the Christian faith. Yet it seems to be something more than a coincidence that in the region in which, beginning not far from the ninth or tenth century, Christianity had the freest course, that culture developed which by its striking attainments eventually, in the nineteenth and twentieth centuries, led the human race. If it be said that this position was due to the Graeco-Roman heritage, one must recall that the Moslem world was also an heir of Greece and Rome and that from it issued no comparable achievements. The most obvious difference in the ingredients of the two was that one had Christianity and the other Islam. If it be claimed that the cause must be sought in race, one recalls how varied was Western Europe racially and how some of its greatest accomplishments were from stocks very similar to those in some of the Moslem lands and certainly not much different from those in the Byzantine East which, though officially Christian, did not give the faith as free course as did the West. If climate be put forward as the explanation, some other portions of the globe with almost the same conditions have had a vastly different cultural record. Christianity was undoubtedly a factor. It seems to have been the ingredient without which the distinctive results would not have followed. The foundations for these results were laid before A.D. 1350.[4]

—Kenneth Scott Latourette
Advance Through Storm

C. In more recent centuries

This intensely personal message, however, had social effects which transformed England. "The Gospel of Christ knows of no religion but social," said Wesley, "no holiness but social holiness." Without the evangelical revival there is no explaining John Howard's prison reforms or William Wilberforce's "Go on, in the name of God and in the power of His might, till even American slavery (the vilest that ever saw the sun) shall vanish away before it." A new social conscience was created in England, with results so far-reaching that Lecky attributes England's escape from a French Revolution largely to the evangelical movement, and J. R. Green says that "a religious revival burst forth which changed in a few years the whole temper of English society."[5]

—Harry Emerson Fosdick
Great Voices of the Reformation

D. In Eastern culture

"Only Christ Can Change Men Like That"

In the region around Raghavapuram the Malas had been notorious criminals. The town itself was the headquarters of a robber band, led by a Mala named Venkayya. When this robber chief and many of his followers were converted a mass movement began that has brought many thousands of Malas in that region to Christ. Three miles from Venkayya's home in Raghavapuram is the village of Kammavaram, where live a number of prosperous Kamma families, several of whom have professed the Christian faith and united with the Church. On our way across the fields to the village we overtook one of the Kammas who had not yet become a Christian nor made any move in that direction. We began to converse. "Do you know the Christians of your village?" we asked. "Yes, all of them." "What do you think of them?" "They are our best people." "Are all of them your best people?" "There are only Hindus and Christians in the village and the Christians are much better than we Hindus." "Do you mean that even the Mala Christians are better than you Hindus?" "Oh yes, some of them are not as good as others, but as a whole they are better than we are." "Has being Christians made them better?" "Certainly! Before they became Christians they were robbers and murderers. Even we Kammas were afraid of them. The difference between them as they were then and as they are now is like that between the earth and the sky, between noon-day and night." "What other groups have become Christians?" "Two lower Sudra groups." "Are their lives also changing?" "Yes, in just the same way. Some were drunkards, now they don't drink." "And what of your people? Haven't some of them become Christians?" "Yes." "Are they also being changed?" "Yes, and more rapidly than the others were. It seems that we Kammas are better material than the Malas, but none of our people would have become Christians if they had not first seen what happened to the Malas."

"You say that you have seen many bad men changed to good men, drunkards to sober men, robbers to honest neighbors. Has that happened only to those who have become Christians? Haven't you seen any one changed like that in Hinduism?"

At this the old man seemed surprised that we should ask such a question and revealed how deeply he had been affected by what he had seen. "Never. Only Christ can change men like that." A few months later the old man and his entire family knelt before the altar in the little Church in the village and, after confessing their faith, received the sacred rite of baptism, and were admitted to the Church.[6]

—J. Waskom Pickett
Christ's Way to India's Heart

★ ★ ★ ★ ★

1. As this small sampling suggests, the traditional Christian approach to social problems is the conversion of individuals who in turn bring their new insights to bear on their society. This has been a slow but a certain process. In today's rapidly changing society is this method adequate?

2. The church has been criticized for stressing individual salvation instead of social reform. Is the criticism justified?

3. What should be the role of the church in America as it deals with obvious social injustice?

4. How would you define the role of the church in a revolutionary period? Should it resist, encourage, or promote social programs to foster equality, justice, and adequate food, housing, and welfare for all people?

46: THE ROLE OF THE MISSIONARY IN REVOLUTION

A. The missionary as revolutionary

The missionary task is a revolutionary task. Its message, the Christian gospel, has been the most revolutionary force in history. That message of God's love and, as a result, of human dignity and freedom and equality has awakened the longings which lie behind so many of the current revolutions. The proclamation of that message, in word and deed, involves one in the mainstream of today's world. And the missionary task is a Christian task. It has an evangelistic purpose, accepting the deepest opportunity and obligation of the Christian faith—to witness to what God in Jesus Christ has done. It involves one in the "incarnational life"—to go to another people, identify with them, suffer for and with them, live the "servant life" in their midst, and offer oneself as an instrument of God's love.[7]

—T. Watson Street
On the Growing Edge of the Church

B. The missionary vs. the economic exploiter

Missionaries were often the first to enter after the way had been prepared, but thereafter, being men and women of singleness of purpose and without thought of gain, they pursued a policy that soon lined them up beside the people whom they had come to serve and against the agents of business and government who were there for other purposes. The missionary was usually the only representative of disinterested good will, and although he did not—in fact could not—divest himself of his own national and cultural associations he stood as a "third force" in the long struggle for nationhood and independence which the peoples of the non-Christian world have waged for the past century.

* * * * *

The missionary alone cannot accept the blame for the cultural dislocations and disturbances that have taken place in the non-Christian world. The missionary movement, as we have seen, was part of the expansive movement of Western mechanized civilization into the rest of the world. The missionary was not the only influence at work. His policies were often shortsighted. He brought with him the cultural forms of his own people. But there were other agencies introducing other aspects of Western culture to the East and Africa.

The trader brought to the people of the non-Western world the West's machines and gadgets, new kinds of cloth and clothing, new foods and drink, new methods of amusement. To secure a market he popularized new vices and created new appetites. Industry, by attracting villagers and tribespeople to mines and factories, infected them with new and disruptive habits, dangerous diseases, and explosive ideas that were bound to revolutionize the cultural pattern from which they came. Public transportation, by crowding people indiscriminately into trains and buses, has been a powerful force in breaking down class and caste distinctions. The popularity of the Western motion picture and recorded music and, with literates, of newspapers, novels, and magazines, has disseminated a distorted version of Western culture that appealed to many, disgusted some, and influenced everyone who came in touch with them. As the early missionary was shocked by the nakedness of the "heathen," so the traditional father or mother in the Orient and Africa stands aghast at short skirts, bathing costumes, and sexual promiscuity as revealed by these interpreters of Western "culture." And well they may be!

Culture diffusion has become world-wide. No part of the world has been completely isolated from the forces that, for better or worse, have been making the world a unity. These forces are having a revolutionizing effect on the ancient cultures and tribal patterns of the rest of the world. It is a testimony to their cohesiveness and to the good that inheres in them that they have been able to withstand this onslaught. Individualism, imperialism, materialism, industrialization, modernization, ultra-nationalism—all of which are Western imports—are shaking these civilizations and cultures and in some cases causing them to crack.

But the missionary has stood almost alone in bringing another set of cultural values—humanitarianism, co-operation, disinterested service, racial equality, respect for personality—which have served to interpret the better aspects of the West to the rest of the world. He has, in fact, protected native peoples from the worst aspects of the culture he represents. He has been a buffer, a conserver, not a disturber. In the cautious words of a professional sociologist,

whatever other good or harm he [the missionary] has done to alien cultures through zeal or ignorance, he has brought certain elements of his own culture which have counteracted other influences. This has served, in some degree, to give protection to the peoples of the alien cultures against the unchecked operations of economic motives or imperialistic ambitions. . . . The trader is not always devoid of religion or ethics, nor is the missionary always immune to economic temptation. But institutionally he is a necessary counterpart to the institutional behavior of the trader or the administrator in the total process of cultural diffusion. (G. Gordon Brown, "Missions and Cultural Diffusion," in *American Journal of Sociology,* November, 1944, p. 217)[8]

—Willis Church Lamott
Revolution in Missions

C. The missionary's higher calling

If the missionary does not have for his basic objective the social, political and economic goals, what does he have in mind and how is he oriented to his work? Missions is a religious or spiritual business which governs the whole man. Missions is the product of the conviction that Christianity is the divine life in man and it is designed to bring men that life. Despite accusations of proselyting, and fanaticism, the aim of missions is to bring men divine life. While it is pleasant to feed the hungry, heal the sick, and bind up the wounds of the fallen, these are not in themselves the aim of missions. Methods cannot be confused with the aim nor shall methods he allowed tu become the aim or to usurp the aim the missionary has in mind. By that is meant that philanthropy, however good it may be, ought not to supplant the real reason for being there. Nor ought the church to retain outworn methods which have demonstrated their own ineffectiveness in doing what it thinks to be its primary work.[9]

—Harold Lindsell
Missionary Principles and Practice

★ ★ ★ ★ ★

1. The above statements suggest that the missionary who pursues his higher calling will find revolution a by-product of his efforts. Do you agree?

2. Should the church support missionaries whose primary task is agricultural, educational, or medical? What is the purpose for these kinds of missionary activity?

3. Should missionaries actively collaborate with nationals in political matters, either pro-government or pro-revolution?

4. How active should American ministers and churches be in protest demonstrations, political parties, and community projects?

5. Lesslie Newbigin's statement may be helpful here. What do you think of it? "The preaching of the Gospel and the service of men's needs are equally authentic and essential parts of the Church's responsibility. But neither is a substitute for the other. No amount of service, however expert and however generous, is a substitute for the explicit testimony to Jesus Christ . . . There is no equivalent to the name of Jesus. But equally, the preaching of that Name will be empty if he who speaks it is not willing to deal honestly and realistically with the issues that his hearers have to face." (See "From the Editor," *International Review of Missions,* Vol. LIV, No. 216, October, 1965, p. 422.)

47: THE CHURCH AND THE CLASSLESS SOCIETY

A. Does conversion improve social attitudes?

"Has the conversion of these upper caste men and women improved their attitudes toward you?" we asked hundreds of Christians of out-caste origin. Without exception they replied affirmatively. Asked how the improved attitudes were expressed, many gave impressive replies. "They recognize now that we, too, are men and some of those who formerly oppressed us now treat us as blood brothers," said one grey-haired deacon. His nephew illuminated that comment as follows: "Do you recall the rich farmer with whom you talked this morning? Last year he kicked me three times because I complained that his cattle had damaged one of my crops. Then he became a Christian and came to our house to ask forgiveness. And when a Brahman struck my mother last month because she didn't come to his house when sent for, although she explained that her baby was ill and she couldn't leave him, that farmer rebuked the Brahman and threatened to prosecute him, if he should ever mistreat any of us again."[10]

—J. Waskom Pickett
Christ's Way to India's Heart

B. The Church did not conduct an egalitarian campaign to eradicate classes.

Apparently its leaders entertained no thought of erasing the social distinctions which characterized the Empire, and especially the Empire in the years in which Christianity was becoming numerically dominant. Yet here, too, by proclaiming that all Christians were heirs of eternal life and that worldly position did not control eternal destiny, it released ideas which, centuries later, had marked influence in breaking down stratifications in society.[11]

—Kenneth Scott Latourette
The First Five Centuries

C. A second kind of improvement, which I am calling "lift," is due to church and mission activities.

The congregation and its members have the great benefit of medicine, education, loving friendship, and protection. The founding mission or Church establishes schools, hospitals, agricultural centers, literacy classes, and many other institutions to serve and help the general public and specially the new brothers in Christ. If these are illiterate, they are taught to read. Their children, attending church and mission schools—or, increasingly, tax-supported schools—become grade-school, high-school, and college graduates. Perhaps they go to Christian vocational schools and become mechanics, radio technicians, or artisans. Girls, sent to nurses' or teachers' training schools, are snapped up by the rapidly expanding government health and education programs and get good salaries. Able men

241

and women rise to positions of international note in the Churches. A few or many, depending on the country, enter government service and hold positions of influence. The wealth of Christians rises. They become middle-class people. Members of the Christian community who have not personally done so well, nevertheless share in the general sense of well-being. All this I am calling "lift."[12]

—Donald A. McGavran
Understanding Church Growth

* * * * *

1. *Lift*, as described by McGavran, sounds beneficial to American ears. What could possibly be wrong with something which sounds so right?

2. Compare Selection B with A and C. Latourette (in B) is discussing Christianity's earliest centuries. Are the results of this teaching to be found in A and C? What then should be the Christian attitude toward caste or class distinctions now, since Latourette seems to suggest that Christian ideas need "centuries" to become effective? Can we afford to wait?

3. According to what you now know of church growth thought, what would be this school of thought's attitude toward the importance of promoting a classless society?

48: CHANGED INDIVIDUALS CHANGE SOCIETIES

The Conversion of a Brahman

A Brahman, recently converted told us that he was led to Christ by the discovery that his servant, whom he had despised as an out-caste, was, in fact, more honourable and worthy of respect than he himself. Here is the Brahman's story:

"One night during the harvest season I was in my field guarding my crops. A few nights before thieves had cut and stolen nearly a half acre of grain. My Madiga servant, a boy of about 18, was with me. I became hungry and told the lad to steal some fruit from a neighbor's tree. He politely declined saying that he could not steal. I ridiculed the idea that any Madiga would object to stealing and when he persisted in refusing I grew angry and ordered him to bring me the fruit without delay. When he again declined, I struck him and he ran away. Then I went to my neighbour's tree and helped myself. Shortly after this I started around the field ashamed of what I had done. Gradually it dawned on me that I was a thief as truly as were the men who had stolen my grain. And I had struck my servant because he would not steal. I wished the lad were back, and I debated whether I should go to the village and call him, also whether I should tell him that I was sorry I had struck him. In the field, alone at midnight, I was frightened. Just then I heard his voice. It came from under a tree some distance away. I went nearer to listen, supposing he was telling some one what I had done. But he was apparently alone. He was praying. After a while I heard him say, 'Forgive my master, Lord. He doesn't know how to overcome temptation. His gods don't help him, and, he doesn't understand that he should serve Thee.' That made me thoroughly ashamed. I tried to be angry with him for praying for me. I was humiliated that a Madiga should think he was in a better relation to God than I, a Brahman. But in my heart I knew it was true. I walked away, emboldened by the knowledge that the lad was near. A little later he rejoined me. In a few days I began studying Christianity with the result that I am now a Christian. I found that many of the Madigas are better men than I have ever been, and my old feeling of contempt for the Depressed Classes has changed into a feeling of respect and love."[13]

—J. Waskom Pickett
Christ's Way to India's Heart

Great difficulty was experienced by the constitutional lawyers of Japan when the new order was introduced because there was no suitable word in Japanese to express the idea of human rights. It had come as part of the Western tradition, deriving its

main power from that valuation of the individual which the West learned from the Christian Gospel.[14]

—Lesslie Newbigin
A Faith for This One World?

* * * * *

"We must lay aside all feelings of superiority of culture, race, or nation." Evangelicals agree entirely that the missionary must renounce all pride in *his* personal, racial, or national attributes. He has nothing but what God has given him and there is no scientific reason to judge his race superior to all others. All feelings of white superiority, American superiority, Japanese superiority, or high caste superiority are sinful. All such pride and arrogance must go.

But there is one point at which evangelicals demur. The *treasure* we have (in admittedly earthen vessels) *is* superior to everything which natural man possesses, whether he be white, brown, yellow, or red. It is at this point that D. T. Niles' famous statement errs. Once the beggar has found food, he is no longer hungry; once he has found the treasure he is no longer a beggar. The Galilean Peter remains a Galilean peasant, true; but in Christ he is one of a chosen race, a royal priesthood, a holy nation. He *has come out.* To commend Christ to others, he must not falsely maintain that he is still in darkness. Is the Christian not in danger of being hypocritical if he protests that he is just one beggar telling another where to find food? How to separate the treasure from the vessel and how to speak of the vessel as we should without demeaning the treasure—that is the problem here.[15]

—Donald McGavran
Eye of the Storm

* * * * *

1. Can there be a real classless society without changing individual attitudes first?

2. Marxism has made great strides in this century by up-lifting the lower classes and promising a society without class distinction. What is the Christian alternative to communism?

3. Does what MoGavran calls *lift* [see Unit 47] create a new elite in society, thereby separating Christians from non-Christians in economic as well as religious ways?

4. What implications does McGavran's *lift* have for American churches? Is it a barrier to evangelism?

49: THE NEW WORLD

The essential elements in the new situation are as follows:

1. The political domination of the world by the white races has ended. The course of history is no longer determined by decisions made in the Western capitals. Western culture as a whole is no longer accepted by the rest of the world as that which has the right and power to dominate and replace the cultures of Asia and Africa.

2. There is emerging a single world culture which has its characteristic expression in the rapidly growing cities in all parts of the world, and which has as its common substance the science and technology which have been developed in the West, and as its driving power the belief in the possibility of rational planning for total human welfare. This world culture is made possible by the existence of modern means of communication and transport.

3. The Christian church is now, for the first time, no longer confined to a small part of the earth, but is present—normally as a small minority—in almost all parts of the inhabited world.[16]

—Lesslie Newbigin
A Faith for This One World?

If Lesslie Newbigin is correct in these three elements of the new world, one project remains to be completed. On the basis of your study of church growth thought as introduced in this volume, prepare your set of recommendations to reshape the missions and evangelism programs of your church in order to insure the growth of the world-wide church of Jesus Christ in the twenty-first century.

APPENDIX

THE CHURCH GROWTH MOVEMENT

Herbert Works

Ralph Waldo Emerson once said, "An institution is the lengthened shadow of one man." His words could easily have referred to the Institute of Church Growth. The man is Donald Anderson McGavran. Donald A. McGavran is a veteran of thirty years of missionary service with the United Christian Missionary Society in India. His pioneering concepts about the underlying dynamics of church growth began to take shape in the 1930's when he was secretary-treasurer of his mission. Two things in particular made a deep impression on him. One was the vast sum of money required to maintain the mission as compared with the relatively small number of additions to the church resulting from the investment. The other impression was made by the remarkable movements to Christ among the outcaste and lower caste peoples of India. McGavran became convinced that the missionary force could be prepared and employed to encourage these "people movements to Christ." In 1955, after a fruitful association with J. Waskom Pickett in analyzing the mass movements in India, McGavran wrote *Bridges of God: A Study in the Strategy of Missions.* India was not the only country experiencing people movements, nor was McGavran the only observer. He was the one, however, who pursued these observations to fruitful development, and his book has become a missiological classic.

From 1955 to 1960 McGavran refined these ideas. Still with the U.C.M.S., he traveled to Puerto Rico, the Philippines, Thailand, and elsewhere to observe the work of U.C.M.S. missionaries. These were often painful times for him, since concepts clearly valid in India did not always apply to other parts of the world. They needed to be refined if they were to have universal application.

From this research a dream grew. McGavran envisioned an institute to which missionaries of all denominations could come during a furlough year, armed with accurate data from their fields, prepared to analyze the causes for growth and non-growth among their people. When no significant response came from McGavran's overtures to Disciples of Christ seminaries, Ross J. Griffeth, President of Northwest Christian College in Eugene, Oregon, offered to work with him in developing the Institute of Church Growth.

The I.C.G. opened its doors in January, 1961. Its facilities, staff, and student body were small. Bookshelves had been cleared out of an area of the third floor stacks of the college library to make room for the Institute. McGavran was the sole instructor, and his one student was Keith Hamilton, a Methodist missionary from Bolivia. There were no telephone, no secretary, and very little budget.

During the four and one-half years at Northwest Christian College, although the Institute could offer no degree, some sixty students studied with McGavran. These represented twenty-four countries and fifteen different mission boards or sponsoring agencies. Two lectureships were held featuring mission leaders of renown. McGavran's teaching load was lightened by part-time instruction by two Research Fellows, Alan R. Tippett and George Martindale. During this period in Eugene, the influence of church growth thinking spread rapidly. McGavran was much sought after as a lecturer, particularly among evangelicals. Beginning in 1963, the Evangelical Foreign Missions Association sponsored an annual Church Growth Seminar at Winona Lake. He spoke to a conference on church growth under the auspices of the World Council of Churches at Iberville in 1963. He conducted seminars in Mexico City, Brazil, and Central America. He spoke every free Sunday to some congregation about God's concern that the lost be found. The influence of the movement spread through prolific writings. McGavran wrote articles, letters to editors, book reviews, and books. In 1964, Overseas Crusades began to publish the *Church Growth Bulletin,* edited by McGavran. In addition, McGavran was demanding of the Research Fellows careful writing, anticipating that most of the research of the I.C.G. would be published. The first book by a student was Hamilton's *Church Growth in the High Andes.*

Success strained the relationship between the Institute of Church Growth and Northwest Christian College, since more and more funds were needed to care for the increasing number of students interested in working under McGavran. The solution came in 1965 when Fuller Theological Seminary in Pasadena, California, invited the institute to move to the seminary and to receive academic standing as a School of World Mission, along with the School of Theology and School of Psychology. Northwest Christian College, with mixed emotions, agreed to this proposal.

Since the move to Fuller Theological Seminary, the Institute of Church Growth has expanded at an almost explosive rate. By 1974, there were six full-time faculty members aided by visiting professors. SWM has become the center for the development of the new discipline of missiology. Two Masters degrees are offered as well as a doctorate in missiology. In the 1973-74 academic year, 120 were enrolled. Since 1963, 37 books have been published by research associates, and 86 other unpublished theses, dissertations, and independent studies were completed. In 1969, more than half the missions graduate theses reported to Missionary Research Library came from the Fuller School of World Missions. The faculty members have written extensively and are considered by church leaders around the world to be key resource persons in the field of missions.

NOTES

Notes to Chapter 1

1 Kenneth Scott Latourette, *Advance Through Storm* (New York: Harper and Row, Publishers, 1945), pp. 418-419.

2 Roland Allen, *The Spontaneous Expansion of the Church* (Grand Rapids, Michigan: William B. Eerdmans Publishing Company, 1962), p. 7. Copyright by World Dominion Press.

3 Stephen Neill, *A History of Christian Missions* (Baltimore, Maryland: Penguin Books, © Stephen Neill 1964), p. 26.

4 Allen, *The Spontaneous Expansion*, p. 49.

5 Kenneth Scott Latourette, *The First Five Centuries* (New York: Harper and Brothers Publishers, 1937), p. 114.

6 *Ibid.*, p. 117.

7 *Ibid.*, pp. 162-168.

8 Neill, *A History of Christian Missions*, pp. 79-80.

9 Kenneth Scott Latourette, *The Thousand Years of Uncertainty* (New York: Harper and Brothers, 1938), pp. 205-206.

10 *Ibid.*, p. 17.

11 Neill, *A History of Christian Missions*, pp. 68-69. This letter was addressed not directly to Augustine but to the abbot Mellitus, who was on his way to Britain and was instructed to convey the contents to Augustine.

12 J. Herbert Kane, *A Global View of Christian Missions From Pentecost to the Present* (Grand Rapids, Michigan: Baker Book House, 1971), pp. 73-75.

13 Neill, *A History of Christian Missions*, pp. 333-334.

14 *Ibid.*, p. 263.

15 Lesslie Newbigin, *A Faith for This One World?* (London: SCM Press Ltd., 1961), pp. 10-11.

16 Roland Allen, ed. David M. Paton, *The Ministry of the Spirit* (Grand Rapids, Michigan: William B. Eerdmans Publishing Co., 1960), p. 76. Copyright by World Dominion Press.

17 *Life of Swami Vivekananda*, 5th impression (Calcutta: Advaita Ashrama, 1955), pp. 514-515, quoted in Stephen Neill, *Call to Mission* (Philadelphia: Fortress Press, 1970), p. 6.

18 R. Pierce Beaver, *The Missionary Between the Times* (Garden City, New York: Doubleday and Company, Inc., 1968), p. 130.

19 Eric S. Fife and Arthur F. Glasser, *Missions in Crisis* (Chicago: Inter-Varsity Press, 1961), pp. 121-122.

Notes to Chapter 2

1 Mme. E. Gouzee, "Counterpoint," Donald McGavran, ed., *Eye of the Storm* (Waco, Texas: Word Books, 1972), p. 161.

2 Emil Brunner, *The Word and the World*, 2nd ed. (London, 1932), p. 108. Quoted in McGavran, ed., *Eye of the Storm*, p. 83.

3 Arthur F. Glasser, "Church Growth Theology," p. 1. Unpublished manuscript.

4 Roland Allen, *Missionary Methods: St. Paul's or Ours?* (Grand Rapids, Michigan: William B. Eerdmans Publishing Co., 1962), p. 90. Copyright by World Dominion Press.

[5] Arthur F. Glasser, "Church Growth and Theology," A. R. Tippett, ed., *God, Man and Church Growth* (Grand Rapids, Michigan: William B. Eerdmans Publishing Co., 1973), p. 52.

[6] Donald McGavran, ed., *Church Growth and Christian Mission* (New York: Harper and Row, Publishers, 1965), pp. 31-32.

[7] Stephen C. Neill, *Creative Tension* (London: Edinburgh House Press, 1959), p. 81.

[8] Donald A. McGavran, *Understanding Church Growth* (Grand Rapids, Michigan: Eerdmans Publishing Company, 1970), p. 34.

[9] Donald A. McGavran, "Social Justice and Evangelism," *World Vision* (June 1965).

[10] Hendrik Kraemer, *The Christian Message in a Non-Christian World* (Grand Rapids, Michigan: Kregel Publications, 1961), p. 60.

[11] McGavran, ed., *Church Growth and Christian Mission,* p. 19.

[12] J. Waskom Pickett, *The Dynamics of Church Growth* (Nashville: Abingdon Press, 1963), pp. 88-89.

[13] Donald McGavran, "Church Growth Movement," p. 9. Paper presented at the Eleventh Biennial Meeting of the Association of Professors of Missions, 1972.

[14] McGavran, *Understanding Church Growth,* p. 46.

[15] McGavran, *How Churches Grow* (New York: Friendship Press, 1966), p. 66.

[16] McGavran, "Church Growth Movement," pp. 11-12.

[17] Allen, *Missionary Methods: St. Paul's or Ours?* pp. 75-76.

[18] McGavran, *How Churches Grow,* p. 14.

[19] McGavran, "Church Growth Movement," p. 12.

[20] Newbigin, *A Faith for This One World?,* pp. 110-111.

[21] Donald McGavran, *The Bridges of God* (New York: Friendship Press, 1955), p. 105.

[22] Louis J. Luzbetak, *The Church and Cultures* (Techny, Illinois: Divine Word Publications, 1963), pp. 17-18.

[23] McGavran, "Church Growth Movement," p. 13.

[24] Peter Wagner, "Pragmatic Strategy for Tomorrow's Mission," Tippett, ed., *God, Man and Church Growth,* pp. 146-147.

[25] McGavran, "Church Growth Movement," pp. 33-34.

[26] Wagner, "Pragmatic Strategy for Tomorrow's Mission," Tippett, ed., *God, Man and Church Growth,* p. 147.

Notes to Chapter 3

[1] McGavran, *Understanding Church Growth,* p. 107.

[2] Luzbetak, *The Church and Cultures,* pp. 60-61.

[3] Harold W. Fehderau, "Missionary Endeavor and Anthropology," *Practical Anthropology,* Vol. 8, No. 5 (September-October), 221-222.

[4] Luzbetak, *The Church and Cultures,* p. 68.

[5] William A. Smalley, "Anthropological Study and Missionary Scholarship," *Practical Anthropology,* Vol. 7, No. 3 (May-June), 119-121.

[6] Donald McGavran, Ed., *Church Growth Bulletin,* VOLUME I-V (South Pasadena, California: William Carey Library, 1969), p. 350.

[7] Kenneth N. Taylor, "Is Polygamy Ever Permissible?" *Eternity Magazine* (July, 1968).

[8] McGavran, ed., *Church Growth Bulletin*, VOLUME I-V, p. 350.

[9] *Ibid.*, pp. 358-359.

[10] *Ibid.*, pp. 352-353.

[11] Roy E. Shearer, "The Psychology of Receptivity and Church Growth," Tippett, ed., *God, Man and Church Growth*, pp. 160-163.

[12] McGavran, ed., *Church Growth and Christian Mission*, p. 71.

[13] *Ibid.*, pp. 78-80.

[14] Gilbert W. Olson, *Church Growth in Sierra Leone* (Grand Rapids, Michigan: William B. Eerdmans Publishing Company, 1969), pp. 50-61.

[15] Eugene A. Nida, "Culture and Church Growth," McGavran, ed., *Church Growth and Christian Mission*, pp. 94-95.

[16] A. R. Tippett, *Church Growth and the Word of God: The Biblical Basis of the Church Growth Viewpoint* (Grand Rapids, Michigan: William B. Eerdmans Publishing Company, 1970), pp. 29-30.

[17] McGavran, *Understanding Church Growth*, p. 85.

[18] *Ibid.*, pp. 193-194.

[19] *Ibid.*, p. 192.

[20] Joseph Conrad Wold, *God's Impatience in Liberia* (Grand Rapids, Michigan: William B. Eerdmans Publishing Company, 1968), pp. 130-131.

[21] McGavran, *Understanding Church Growth*, pp. 190-191.

Notes to Chapter 4

[1] McGavran, *Understanding Church Growth*, pp. 83-84.

[2] McGavran, *Church Growth in Jamaica* (Lucknow, India: Lucknow Publishing House, 1962), pp. iii-iv.

[3] McGavran, *Understanding Church Growth*, p. 155.

[4] *Ibid.*

[5] Tetsunao Yamamori, "Applying the Comparative Method to Church Growth Studies," Tippett, ed., *God, Man and Church Growth*, p. 380.

[6] *Ibid.*, pp. 381-382.

[7] Eugene Nida, "Ideological Conflicts," McGavran, ed., *Church Growth and Christian Mission*, p. 57.

[8] McGavran, *Understanding Church Growth*, p. 92.

[9] Donald A. McGavran and Win Arn, *How to Grow a Church* (Glendale, California: A Division of G/L Publications, 1973), pp. 57-60.

Notes to Chapter 5

[1] William R. Read, *New Patterns of Church Growth in Brazil* (Grand Rapids: William B. Eerdmans Publishing Company, 1965), p. 23.

[2] *Ibid.*, pp. 26-31.

[3] *Ibid.*, pp. 40-43.

[4] McGavran, *How Churches Grow*, pp. 58-59.

[5] McGavran, *The Bridges of God*, pp. 17-18, 21.

[6] Leon Strunk, "The Relationship Web of the Extended Family," McGavran, ed., *Church Growth Bulletin*, Volumes I-V, pp. 106-107.

[7] R. K. Strachan, *The Inescapable Calling* (Grand Rapids, Michigan: William B. Eerdmans Publishing Company, 1968), p. 108.

[8] A. R. Tippett, *Verdict Theology in Missionary Theory* (Lincoln, Illinois: Lincoln Christian College Press, 1969), p. 8.

[9] McGavran, *How Churches Grow,* p. 126.

[10] Charles Bennett, *Tinder in Tabasco* (Grand Rapids, Michigan: William B. Eerdmans Publishing Company, 1968), p. 100.

[11] Charles W. Iglehart, *A Century of Protestant Christianity in Japan* (Rutland, Vermont: Charles E. Tuttle Company, 1959), p. 72.

[12] *Ibid.,* p. 73.

[13] Otis Cary, *A History of Christianity in Japan,* Vol. 2 (New York: Fleming H. Revell Company, 1909), p. 171. Doshisha, located in Kyoto, is a school originally related to the Congregational Church founded in 1875.

[14] *Ibid.*

[15] *Ibid.,* p. 172.

[16] Iglehart, *A Century of Protestant Christianity,* p. 73.

[17] Isamu Yoneda, *Nakada Jyuji Den* (Tokyo: Nakada Jyuji Den Kanko Kai, 1959), p. 303. The title may be translated into English as "Biography of Nakada."

[18] *Ibid.,* pp. 418-429.

[19] Tetsunao Yamamori, "The Doshisha and Holiness Church Revivals," Donald McGavran, ed., *Church Growth Bulletin,* Vol. VIII, No. 3 (January 1972), 195-198.

[20] McGavran, *Understanding Church Growth,* p. 163.

[21] Richard S. Armstrong, *The Oak Lane Story* (New York: Division of Evangelism, Board of National Missions, United Presbyterian Church in the U.S.A., 1971), pp. 13-16, 18-20, 24.

[22] Roger S. Greenway, "Urbanization and Missions," Donald McGavran, ed., *Crucial Issues in Missions Tomorrow* (Chicago: Moody Press, 1972), p. 227.

[23] McGavran, *Understanding Church Growth,* pp. 285-293.

[24] C. Peter Wagner, *Frontiers in Missionary Strategy* (Chicago: Moody Press, 1971), pp. 189-197.

[25] Keith E. Hamilton, *Church Growth in the High Andes* (Lucknow, U.P., India: Lucknow Publishing House, 1962), pp. 41-46.

[26] *Ibid.,* pp. 106-114.

[27] McGavran, *Understanding Church Growth,* pp. 346-347.

Notes to Chapter 6

[1] McGavran, *Understanding Church Growth,* pp. 141-142.

[2] McGavran, *The Bridges of God,* p. 109.

[3] J. W. Pickett, W. L. Warnshuis, G. H. Singh, and D. A. McGavran, *Church Growth and Group Conversion* (Lucknow, U.P., India: Lucknow Publishing House, 1956), pp. 21-22, 28-30.

[4] Donald McGavran, John Huegel, and Jack Taylor, *Church Growth in Mexico* (Grand Rapids, Michigan: William B. Eerdmans Publishing Company, 1963). pp. 15, 17, 43-51.

[5] Stan Shewmaker, *Tonga Christianity* (South Pasadena, California: William Carey Library, 1970), pp. 99-102, 104, 106-114.

Notes to Chapter 7

1 Willis Church Lamott, *Revolution in Missions* (New York: The MacMillan Company, © 1954 by Willis Church Lamott), p. 4.

2 J. Bavinck, *An Introduction to the Science of Missions,* trans. David Hugh Freeman, (Philadelphia: The Presbyterian and Reformed Publishing Company, 1960), p. 62.

3 Quoted in Alan Tippett, *Verdict Theology in Missionary Theory,* p. 132.

4 James A. Scherer, *Missionary, Go Home!* (Englewood Cliffs, N. J.: Prentice Hall, Inc., © 1964), p. 79.

5 Tippett, *Verdict Theology,* pp. 142-143.

6 Scherer, *Missionary, Go Home!,* p. 95.

7 George W. Peters, *Mission-Church Relationship I,* Bibliotheca Sacra, CXXV (July 1968) 499, pp. 205-215.

8 Minutes of National Executive Committee of the Congo Protestant Council, June 1-4, 1969, IV Resolutions.

0 Peters, *Ibid.,* p. 214.

10 Peters, *Mission-Church Relationship II,* Bibliotheca Sacra, CXXV (October 1968) 500, pp. 302-303.

11 T. Watson Street, *On the Growing Edge of the Church* (Richmond, Virginia: John Knox Press, 1965), pp. 25-38.

12 Alfred Larson, "Church-Mission Relationship—A Fused Partnership," Vergil Gerber, ed., *Missions in Creative Tension* (South Pasadena, California: William Carey Library, 1971), pp. 46-48.

13 Louis L. King, "Church-Mission Relationships Overseas," Gerber, ed., *Missions in Creative Tension,* p. 174.

14 *Ibid.,* pp. 174-175.

15 Beaver, *The Missionary Between the Times,* p. 143.

16 *Ibid.,* p. 151.

17 Neill, *A History of Christian Missions,* p. 512.

18 Harold Lindsell, *Missionary Principles and Practice* (Westwood, New Jersey: Fleming H. Revell Company, 1955), p. 340.

19 Harold R. Cook, *An Introduction to the Study of Christian Missions* (Chicago: Moody Press, 1954), p. 69.

20 Lindsell, *Missionary Principles and Practice,* pp. 142-143.

21 *Ibid.,* pp. 69-70.

22 Nevin C. Harner and David D. Baker, *Missionary Education in Your Church* (New York: Friendship Press, 1957), p. 34.

23 Lindsell, *Missionary Principles and Practice,* p. 341.

24 Stephen J. Corey, *The Preacher and His Missionary Message* (Nashville: Cokesbury Press, 1930), p. 12.

25 Jack Speer, "Developing a Congregational Mission Program." Unpublished paper prepared at the School of World Mission and Institute of Church Growth, Fuller Theological Seminary. Undated.

26 James G. Van Buren, "The Focal Church in Missions," *Christian Standard* (October 17, 1959), 3-4.

Notes to Chapter 8

1 Eugene L. Smith, *God's Mission—and Ours* (Nashville: Abingdon Press, 1961), pp. 83-84.

2 McGavran, *How Churches Grow*, p. 39.
3 Allen, *Missionary Methods*, p. 49.
4 Melvin L. Hodges, *Growing Young Churches* (Chicago: Moody Press, 1970), p. 74.
5 Sidney Langford, "What About Institutions?" Gerber, ed., *Missions in Creative Tension*, p. 42.
6 Luzbetak, *The Church and Cultures*, p. 204.
7 Louis L. King, "Mission/Church Relations Overseas (Part I: In Principle)," Gerber, ed., *Missions in Creative Tension*, p. 164.
8 Quoted in Neill, *A History of Christian Missions*, p. 367.
9 McGavran, *The Bridges of God*, pp. 139-140.
10 McGavran, *How Churches Grow*, pp. 150-152.
11 This signed document was summarized and edited by Donald McGavran. See *Church Growth Bulletin*, Vol. IX, No. 4 (March 1973), 301-302, 307.
12 Sir George Trevelyan, *Life and Letters of Lord Macaulay* (London: Longmans, 1908), quoted in J. Waskom Pickett, *Christ's Way to India's Heart*, 3rd ed. (Lucknow, India: Lucknow Publishing House, 1960), p. 16.
13 Langford, "What About Institutions?" Gerber, ed., *Missions in Creative Tension*, p. 43.
14 From *Church Growth Bulletin*, Vol. IX, No. 4 (March 1973), 307.
15 George W. Peters, "Mission/Church Relations Overseas (Part II)," Gerber, ed., *Missions in Creative Tension*, pp. 220-222.
16 Scherer, *Missionary, Go Home!*, p. 33.
17 Pickett, *Christ's Way to India's Heart*, p. 35.

Notes to Chapter 9

1 Donald McGavran, "Critique of Harry Partin's Paper on the Gospel and the Non-Christian Religions." A mimeographed paper distributed at the Institute of Church Growth, Northwest Christian College, 1961.
2 At the request of the International Missionary Council, Kraemer wrote *The Christian Message in a Non-Christian World* in order to provide study material for the World Missionary Conference in 1938.
3 Karl Barth, *Church Dogmatics*, Vol. I, Pt. 1 (New York: Charles Scribner's Sons, 1937), pp. 124-125.
4 *Ibid.*, p. 125.
5 *Ibid.*, p. 111.
6 See Kraemer's *Religion and the Christian Faith* (1957) and *Why Christianity of All Religions?* (1962).
7 Hendrik Kraemer, *Why Christianity of All Religions?* Trans. Hubert Hoskins (Philadelphia: The Westminster Press, 1962), p. 116.
8 William E. Hocking, *Living Religions and a World Faith* (New York: The MacMillan Company, 1940), p. 198.
9 Edmund Davison Soper, *The Philosophy of the Christian World Mission* (New York: Abingdon-Cokesbury Press, 1943), pp. 175-176.
10 See *Study Encounter*, Vol. III, No. 2, 1967.
11 Hendrik Kraemer, "Syncretism as a Theological Problem for Missions," Gerald H. Anderson, ed., *The Theology of the Christian Mission* (New York: McGraw-Hill Book Company, Inc., 1961), p. 181.
12 McGavran, *How Churches Grow*, p. 58.

[13] Roy E. Shearer, *Wildfire: Church Growth in Korea* (Grand Rapids, Michigan: William B. Eerdmans Publishing Company, 1966), p. 217.

[14] McGavran, *How Churches Grow,* p. 45.

[15] Lamott, *Revolution in Missions,* p. 143.

[16] McGavran, *How Churches Grow,* p. 47.

Notes to Chapter 10

[1] Joseph L. Allen, "The Church and Social Revolution." Lecture presented at senior colloquy at Perkins School of Theology, Southern Methodist University, on September 13, 1967. Unpublished paper.

[2] Kenneth Scott Latourette, *The First Five Centuries,* p. 365.

[3] *Ibid.,* p. 368.

[4] Latourette, *Advance Through Storm,* pp. 431-432.

[5] Harry Emerson Fosdick, *Great Voices of the Reformation* (New York: Modern Library, 1952), p. 496.

[6] Pickett, *Christ's Way to India's Heart,* pp. 41-43.

[7] Street, *On the Growing Edge of the Church,* pp. 83-84.

[8] Lamott, *Revolution in Missions,* pp. 118-120.

[9] Lindsell, *Missionary Principles and Practice,* pp. 166-167.

[10] Pickett, *Christ's Way to India's Heart,* p. 61.

[11] Latourette, *The First Five Centuries,* p. 263.

[12] McGavran, *Understanding Church Growth,* pp. 261-262.

[13] Pickett, *Christ's Way to India's Heart,* pp. 50-51.

[14] Newbigin, *A Faith for This One World?* p. 25.

[15] McGavran, *Eye of the Storm,* p. 210.

[16] Newbigin, *A Faith for This One World?* pp. 108-109.

ACKNOWLEDGMENTS

Acknowledgment is made to the following, who have granted permission for the reprinting of copyrighted material:

William Carey Library, *Church Growth Bulletin,* Vol. I-V, ed. by Donald McGavran, © 1969, by Wm. Carey Library; "What About Institutions?" by Sidney Langford, "Church-Mission Relationship—A Fused Partnership," by Alfred Larson, "Church-Mission Relationships Overseas," by Louis L. King, "Mission/Church Relations Overseas" part II, by George W. Peters, from *Missions in Creative Tension,* ed. by Vergil Gerber, © 1971, Wm. Carey Library; *Tonga Christianity* by Stan Shewmaker, © 1970, by Wm. Carey Library.

Center for Applied Research in the Apostolate, *The Church and Cultures* by Louis J. Luzbetak, © 1963.

Division of Evangelism, Board of National Missions, United Pres. Church in the U.S.A., *The Oak Lane Story* by Richard S. Armstrong, © 1971.

William B. Eerdmans, *Church Growth and the Word of God: The Biblical Basis of the Church Growth Viewpoint* by A. R. Tippett, © 1970, by Wm. B. Eerdmans; *Church Growth in Mexico* by McGavran, Huegel, and Taylor, © 1963, by Wm. B. Eerdmans;

God, Man, and Church Growth, ed. by A. R. Tippett, © 1973, by Wm. B. Eerdmans; *God's Impatience in Liberia* by Joseph Conrad Wold, © 1968, by Wm. B. Eerdmans; *Missionary Methods: St. Paul's or Ours?* by Roland Allen, 1962, © by World Dominion Press; *New Patterns of Church Growth in Brazil* by Wm. R. Read, © 1965, by Wm. B. Eerdmans; *The Ministry of the Spirit* by Roland Allen, (ed.) David M. Paton, 1960, © 1962, by World Dominion Press; *The Spontaneous Expansion of the Church* by Roland Allen, © 1962, by Wm. B. Eerdmans; *Understanding Church Growth* by Donald McGavran, © 1970, by Wm. B. Eerdmans.

Friendship Press, *How Churches Grow* by Donald McGavran, © 1966, by Friendship Press; *The Bridges of God* by Donald McGavran, © 1955, by Friendship Press.

Gospel Light Publications, *How to Grow a Church* by Donald McGavran and Win Arn, © 1973, by Gospel Light Publications.

Harper and Row, Publishers, *Advance Through Storm* by Kenneth Scott Latourette, © 1945, by Harper & Row; *Church Growth and Christian Missions* ed. by Donald McGavran, © 1965, by Harper & Row; *The First Five Centuries* by Kenneth Scott Latourette, © 1937, by Harper & Row; *The Thousand Years of Uncertainty* by Kenneth Scott Latourette, © 1938, by Harper & Row.

Lincoln Christian College Press, *Verdict Theology in Missionary Theory* by Alan R. Tippett, © 1969, by Lincoln Christian College Press.

Lucknow Publishing House, *Christ's Way Into India's Heart* by J. Waskom Pickett, © 1960, by Lucknow Publishing House; *Church Growth and Group Conversion* by Pickett, Warnshuis, Singh, and McGavran, © 1956, by Lucknow Publishing House; *Church Growth in the High Andes* by Keith E. Hamilton, © 1962, by Lucknow Publishing House.

MacMillan Publishing Company, Inc., *Revolution in Missions* by Willis Church Lamott, © 1954, by Willis Church Lamott.

Moody Press, *Growing Young Churches* by Melvin L. Hodges, © 1970, by Melvin L. Hodges.

Penguin Books, Ltd., *A History of Christian Missions* by Stephen Neill, © 1964, by Stephen Neill.

Prentice-Hall, Inc., *Missionary, Go Home!* by James A. Scherer, © 1964, by Prentice-Hall, Inc.

SCM Press, Ltd., *A Faith for This One World?* by Lesslie Newbigin, © 1961, by SCM Press, Ltd.

Fleming H. Revell Company, *Missionary Principles and Practice* by Harold Lindsell, © 1955, by Fleming H. Revell Company.

Acknowledgement is also made to the following magazines, papers, and authors for permission to use their material:

Joseph L. Allen, "The Church and Social Revolution," a lecture presented at senior colloquy at Perkins School of Theology, Southern Methodist University, on September 13, 1967.

Church Growth Bulletin, Vol. VIII, No. 3, Donald McGavran, ed., "The Doshisha and Holiness Church Revivals," by Tetsunao Yamamori, January, 1972.

Church Growth Bulletin, Vol. IX, No. 4, Donald McGavran, ed., March, 1973.

Eternity Magazine, "Is Polygamy Ever Permissible?" by Kenneth N. Taylor, July, 1968.

Donald McGavran, "Critique of Harry Partin's Paper on the Gospel and the Non-Christian Religions," a paper distributed at the Institute of Church Growth, Northwest Christian College, 1961; "Church Growth Movement," papers presented at the Eleventh Biennial Meeting of the Association of Professors of Mission, 1972.

Practical Anthropology, Vol. 7, No. 3, (May-June) "Anthropological Study and Missionary Scholarship," by William A. Smalley.

Practical Anthropology, Vol. 8, No. 5, (September-October) "Missionary Endeavor and Anthropology," by Harold W. Fehderau.

Standard Publishing, "The Focal Church in Missions," by James G. Van Buren, from *Christian Standard,* October 17, 1959.

World Vision, "Social Justice and Evangelism," by Donald McGavran, June, 1965.